GRACEFULLY DRESSED

The Modern Woman's Style Guide: From Everyday Chic to Bridal Grandeur

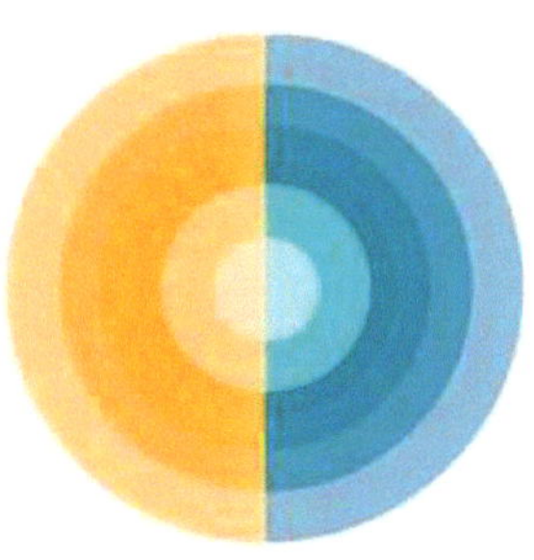

Curating Your Wardrobe for Every Occasion, with Mixfabric

By Gurpuran Singh

Glossary/Index

This glossary provides definitions for key fashion terms and concepts discussed throughout **"GRACEFULLY DRESSED" The Modern Woman's Style Guide: from Everyday Chic to Bridal Grandeur**. Use it as a quick reference to enhance your understanding and navigate the world of style with confidence.

● **A-line:** A silhouette that is fitted at the top and gradually widens towards the hem, forming an "A" shape. Flattering for most body types.

○ **See also:** Dresses, Gowns, Lehengas, Kurtis. (Refer to relevant page numbers: e.g., Chapter 1, p. X; Chapter 3, p. Y)

● **Accessories:** Items worn or carried to complement an outfit, such as jewelry, bags, scarves, belts, and footwear.

○ **See also:** Jewellery, Bags, Footwear, Scarves. (Refer to relevant page numbers: e.g., Chapter 7, p. X)

● **Anarkali:** A traditional Indian dress style featuring a fitted bodice and a long, flowing, frock-style flare from the waist or bust.

○ **See also:** Kurtis, Suits. (Refer to relevant page numbers: e.g., Chapter 4, p. X; Chapter 5, p. Y)

● **Aari Work:** A type of Indian embroidery done with a hooked needle, creating intricate chain stitches. (Refer to relevant page numbers: e.g., Chapter 4, p. X)

● **Bandhani:** A traditional Indian tie-dyeing technique that creates intricate patterns by tying fabric in small knots before dyeing. (Refer to relevant page numbers: e.g., Chapter 4, p. X)

● **Batik:** A wax-resist dyeing technique used to create patterns on fabric, often characterized by a distinctive cracked effect. (Refer to relevant page numbers: e.g., Chapter 4, p. X)

● **Beadwork:** Embellishment technique involving sewing small decorative beads onto fabric (Refer to relevant page numbers: e.g., Chapter 3, p. X)

● **Blazer:** A formal or semi-formal jacket, often worn as part of a suit or to elevate a casual outfit. (Refer to relevant page numbers: e.g., Chapter 2, p. X)

● **Bodycon:** A dress or garment that is fitted and clings tightly to the body's contours. (Refer to relevant page numbers: e.g., Chapter 3, p. X)

● **Brocade:** A richly decorative shuttle-woven fabric, often in silk, featuring raised patterns. (Refer to relevant page numbers: e.g., Chapter 4, p. X)

Glossary/Index

- **Capsule Wardrobe:** A small, curated collection of versatile clothing items that can be mixed and matched to create numerous outfits. (Refer to relevant page numbers: e.g., Chapter 7, p. X)
- **Chikankari:** A delicate and traditional white-on-white (or pastel) embroidery style from Lucknow, India. (Refer to relevant page numbers: e.g., Chapter 4, p. X)
- **Choli:** The fitted blouse worn with a lehenga skirt or saree. (Refer to relevant page numbers: e.g., Chapter 6, p. X)
- **Churidar:** A type of fitted Indian pant that is tight-fitting and gathers at the ankle, forming wrinkle-like pleats. (Refer to relevant page numbers: e.g., Chapter 4, p. X)
- **Cigarette Pants:** Slim-fit trousers that are straight or slightly tapered from the knee down, ending at or just above the ankle. (Refer to relevant page numbers: e.g., Chapter 2, p. X)
- **Co-ord Set (Co-ordinated Set):** Matching top and bottom pieces designed to be worn together, creating a cohesive look.
  - **See also:** Pant Suit, Skirt Suit. (Refer to relevant page numbers: e.g., Chapter 1, p.X; Chapter 3, p. Y)
- **Crepe:** A fabric characterized by a crinkled or pebbled texture, known for its beautiful drape and wrinkle resistance. (Refer to relevant page numbers: e.g., Chapter 2, p. X)
- **Culottes:** Wide-legged trousers that typically end mid-calf or just below the knee. (Refer to relevant page numbers: e.g., Chapter 1, p. X)
- **Cutdana:** Tiny cylindrical beads used for embellishment, often giving a subtle sparkle.(Refer to relevant page numbers: e.g., Chapter 3, p. X)
- **Dabka Work:** A type of raised embroidery using fine coiled metallic threads. (Refer to relevant page numbers: e.g., Chapter 6, p. X)
- **Dhoti Pants:** Traditional Indian pants that are draped and pleated to create a unique, often voluminous, silhouette. (Refer to relevant page numbers: e.g., Chapter 4, p. X)
- **Dupatta:** A long scarf or stole, often an integral part of Indian ethnic suits and lehengas, used for modesty or style.
  - **See also:** Stole, Veil. (Refer to relevant page numbers: e.g., Chapter 4, p. X; Chapter 5, p. Y)
- **Embroidery:** The art of decorating fabric or other materials with needle and thread or yarn. (Refer to relevant page numbers: e.g., Chapter 4, p. X)

Glossary/Index

Glossary/Index

Glossary/Index

Glossary/Index

- **Puja:** A traditional Indian religious ceremony or act of worship. (Refer to relevant page numbers: e.g., Chapter 5, p. X)
- **Rani Haar:** A very long, multi-layered traditional Indian necklace, often extending to the navel. (Refer to relevant page numbers: e.g., Chapter 7, p. X)
- **Resham:** Fine silk thread embroidery, used for intricate and delicate patterns in Indian ethnic wear. (Refer to relevant page numbers: e.g., Chapter 4, p. X)
- **Salwar:** The loose, pleated trousers that form the bottom part of a salwar kameez suit. (Refer to relevant page numbers: e.g., Chapter 4, p. X)
- **Salwar Kameez:** A traditional Indian three-piece suit comprising a kameez (tunic), salwar (bottom), and dupatta (scarf).
  - **See also:** Pant Suit, Palazzo Suit, Sharara Suit, Garara Suit. (Refer to relevant page numbers: e.g., Chapter 4, p. X)
- **Sangeet Ceremony:** A lively pre-wedding ritual in Indian weddings involving music, dance, and celebration. (Refer to relevant page numbers: e.g., Chapter 5, p. X)
- **Saree:** A traditional Indian garment consisting of a long piece of fabric draped around the body in various styles. (Refer to relevant page numbers: e.g., Chapter 5, p. X)
- **Satin:** A fabric weave that creates a smooth, lustrous, and shiny surface. (Refer to relevant page numbers: e.g., Chapter 3, p. X)
- **Sequins:** Small, flat, shiny discs sewn onto fabric for decorative and dazzling effects. (Refer to relevant page numbers: e.g., Chapter 3, p. X)
- **Shapewear:** Undergarments designed to temporarily alter the shape of the body for a smoother silhouette under clothing. (Refer to relevant page numbers: e.g., Chapter 7, p. X)
- **Sharara:** A traditional Indian pant style, fitted at the waist and flaring dramatically from the knee downwards, resembling a skirt. (Refer to relevant page numbers: e.g., Chapter 4, p. X)
- **Sheath Dress/Gown:** A form-fitting dress or gown that is straight and skims the body's silhouette from top to bottom. (Refer to relevant page numbers: e.g., Chapter 3, p. X)
- **Silk:** A natural protein fiber known for its luxurious sheen, soft feel, and strength, used in various forms for Indian ethnic wear. (Refer to relevant page numbers: e.g., Chapter 4, p.X)
- **Slip Dress:** A minimalist, lingerie-inspired dress with thin straps and a fluid drape. (Refer to relevant page numbers: e.g., Chapter 3, p. X)

Glossary/Index

Introduction

GRACEFULLY DRESSED

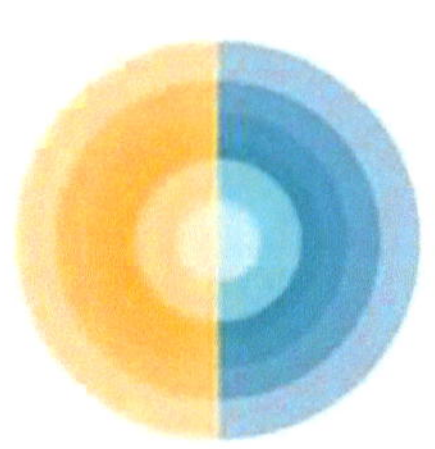

In the vibrant tapestry of a modern woman's life, every day is an occasion, and every occasion demands a unique expression of self. From the quiet comfort of a casual morning to the dazzling grandeur of a wedding celebration, our clothing accompanies us, reflects our mood, and silently narrates our story. But for many, the journey of dressing can feel daunting, a labyrinth of trends, expectations, and choices that often leave us overwhelmed rather than inspired. That's where ***"GRACEFULLY DRESSED"*** **The Modern Woman's Style Guide: From Everyday Chic to Bridal Grandeur** steps in. As **Gurpuran Singh**, the founder of **Mixfabric**, I've poured years of passion and expertise into creating this comprehensive roadmap. This isn't just a book about fashion; it's a guide to understanding your personal style, building a versatile wardrobe, and mastering the art of dressing with confidence and grace for every single moment life throws your way. We believe that true style isn't about chasing fleeting fads; it's about curating a collection of pieces that empower you, celebrate your unique identity, and seamlessly adapt to the diverse roles you play. Within these pages, we'll demystify dress codes, decode silhouettes, and unlock the secrets of fabrics that truly elevate your look. We'll explore the comfort of everyday chic, the authority of power dressing, the allure of celebration wear, and journey deep into the heart of India's rich ethnic heritage, culminating in the breathtaking world of bridal grandeur. And at every step, you'll see how **Mixfabric** stands as your trusted partner, crafting exquisite garments that blend timeless elegance with modern sensibilities, ensuring comfort, quality, and undeniable style. Whether you're refreshing your daily essentials, preparing for a critical boardroom meeting, or dreaming of your perfect wedding ensemble, this guide is designed to empower you. Get ready to transform your wardrobe from a collection of clothes into a powerful tool for self-expression, confidence, and joy. Your journey to impeccable style starts now.

Chapter 1; Decoding Your Everyday Style: The Casual Canvas

The pulse of every modern woman's wardrobe beats in her casual wear. Far from being an afterthought, casual clothing is the bedrock of daily comfort, confidence, and authentic self-expression. It's where practicality meets personal flair, allowing you to navigate your day
with ease while subtly showcasing who you are. This chapter is your definitive guide to understanding, curating, and styling a casual wardrobe that's not just comfortable, but genuinely chic and endlessly versatile.

1.1 The Philosophy of Casual Chic: Comfort Meets Confidence

Casual dressing has evolved. It's no longer about throwing on the first comfortable thing you find; it's about making intentional choices that prioritize both comfort and style. The modern casual aesthetic celebrates ease without sacrificing elegance.

● **Defining Your Comfort Zone:** True comfort comes from understanding your body, your movements, and what fabrics feel good against your skin. It means clothes that don't restrict, chafe, or demand constant adjustment. This foundational comfort allows your confidence to truly shine.

● **The Power of Effortless Style:** "Effortless" doesn't mean "no effort." It means creating a look that appears natural, unforced, and polished without feeling overdone. This comes from smart choices in foundational pieces and thoughtful accessorizing.

● **Versatility as a Core Principle:** Your casual wardrobe should be a highly functional ecosystem. Pieces should be able to mix and match seamlessly, adapting to different casual scenarios with minimal fuss. Think about how a single pair of jeans can go from a coffee run to a casual dinner with just a change of top and accessories.

1.2 Building Blocks: Essential Casual Staples for Every Woman

A strong casual wardrobe is built on a foundation of versatile, high-quality essentials. These are the workhorses that you'll reach for again and again, offering endless styling possibilities.

● **1.2.1 The Quintessential T-shirt Collection:**
○ **Fabric First:** Prioritize 100% cotton, organic cotton, or soft cotton blends (e.g., cotton-modal, cotton-spandex for slight stretch). Look for medium-weight fabrics that aren't too sheer or clingy.
○ **Neckline Variety:**
□ **Crew Neck:** Classic, universally flattering, and great for layering.
□ **V-neck:** Elongates the neck, adds a touch of femininity, and is perfect for showcasing delicate necklaces
□ **Scoop Neck:** Softens the neckline, often flattering for broader shoulders.

□ **Boat Neck:** Elegant and sophisticated, offering a wider neckline.
○ **Color Palette:** Start with neutrals: crisp white, classic black, versatile grey marl, and deep navy. Then, add a few shades that flatter your skin tone and complement your existing wardrobe (e.g., olive green, dusty rose, earthy terracotta).
○ **Fit Matters:** Experiment with fits – classic regular fit, slightly oversized for a relaxed vibe, or a slim fit for layering under jackets.

- **1.2.2 The Indispensable Jeans Portfolio:**
o **The Perfect Fit:** This is paramount. Jeans should fit comfortably around the waist, through the hips, and down the legs without gaping or bunching. Don't be afraid to try on multiple sizes and styles.
o **Wash Wisdom:**
□ **Dark Wash:** Most versatile, easily dressed up, and flattering.
□ **Mid Wash:** Classic everyday, relaxed feel.
□ **Light Wash:** Casual, summery, adds a vintage touch.
□ **Black/Grey Wash:** Modern and chic, excellent for urban casual.
□ **Distressed (Subtly):** For a more edgy, relaxed vibe, but keep it minimal for true versatility.
o **Cut & Silhouette:**
□ **Skinny Jeans:** Remain popular, offering a sleek silhouette, great for tucking into boots.
□ **Straight-Leg Jeans:** Timeless and universally flattering, offering a balanced look.
□ **Bootcut Jeans:** Slightly flared at the bottom, ideal for wearing with boots or heels.
□ **Wide-Leg Jeans:** Trendy and comfortable, offering a relaxed yet dramatic silhouette.

□ **Mom Jeans/Dad Jeans:** High-waisted, relaxed fit through the thigh, tapered or straight leg – for a vintage-inspired, comfortable look.
- **1.2.3 Beyond Denim: Versatile Trousers:**
o **Chinos:** A casual alternative to jeans, often in cotton twill, offering a slightly more polished feel. Great for transitional weather.
o **Linen Pants:** Ideal for warm climates, offering breathability and a relaxed, elegant drape.
o **Relaxed Fit Tailored Pants:** Look for elasticated waistbands or drawstring details for comfort, but with a refined fabric and cut that elevates them beyond sweatpants.
o **Joggers (Styled):** Modern joggers in elevated fabrics (e.g., brushed cotton, Tencel) can be dressed up with a smart top and sneakers or mules for a chic athleisure look.

1.3 The Core of Indian Casual: The Versatile Kurti

The kurti is arguably the most versatile piece in an Indian woman's casual wardrobe. Its adaptability makes it suitable for almost any casual setting.

● **1.3.1 Understanding Kurti Cuts & Styles:**

○ **Straight Cut Kurti:** Clean lines, sleek, and modern. Excellent for pairing with straight pants, cigarette pants, or even jeans.

○ **A-line Kurti:** Flared gently from the waist, offering a universally flattering silhouette. Comfortable and graceful.

○ **Anarkali Kurti (Casual Version):** A more voluminous, flared silhouette from the bust or waist. For casual wear, opt for lighter fabrics (cotton, rayon) and minimal embellishments.

○ **High-Low Kurti:** Shorter at the front, longer at the back, adding a contemporary and playful edge.

○ **Asymmetric Kurti:** Uneven hemlines, creating visual interest and a modern look.

○ **Shirt-Style Kurti:** Resembles a long shirt, often with a collar and button down front. Can be worn as a dress or paired with leggings/pants.

- **1.3.2 Fabrics for Everyday Kurtis:**
  o **Cotton:** The undisputed king for daily wear. Breathable, absorbent, and comfortable in all climates. Look for various weaves like mulmul, cambric, slub cotton.
  o **Rayon/Viscose:** Soft, flowing, and drapes beautifully, offering a silky feel at an affordable price. Excellent for a relaxed yet elegant look.
  o **Linen:** Highly breathable and durable, ideal for hot weather. Embraces a naturally wrinkled texture, which adds to its casual charm.
  o **Blends:** Cotton-linen blends, rayon-cotton blends can offer the best of both worlds in terms of comfort, drape, and wrinkle resistance.
- **1.3.3 Styling Your Everyday Kurti: A Practical Guide:**
  o **Kurti with Jeans:** A classic fusion. A short, straight-cut kurti with skinny or straight-leg jeans offers a contemporary urban look. A longer A-line or high-low kurti pairs well with wider-leg jeans for a bohemian touch.
  o **Kurti with Leggings/Jeggings:** A comfortable and streamlined combination. Ensure the kurti length provides adequate coverage.
  o **Kurti with Palazzos:** Creates a flowy, elegant, and comfortable ensemble. Perfect for a relaxed day out, casual brunch, or travel. Choose palazzos in breathable fabrics like rayon or cotton.
  o **Kurti with Cigarette Pants:** For a slightly more polished casual look, especially with a straight or A-line kurti.
  o **Kurti as a Dress:** Shorter kurtis (tunic length) can be worn as dresses, especially if made from opaque fabric. Pair with sneakers or sandals for a relaxed summer look.
  o **Layering with Kurtis:** Wear an open-front kurti as a lightweight jacket or shrug over a simple camisole and jeans. A fitted kurti can also be layered under a denim jacket or a light cardigan.

1.4 The Rise of Co-ord Sets: Effortless & Chic

Co-ord sets (co-ordinated sets) have surged in popularity for their sheer convenience and inherent style. They offer a complete, cohesive look with minimal effort, making them a casual wardrobe game-changer.

● **1.4.1 What Makes Co-ords So Popular?**

o **Instant Outfit:** No guesswork involved; the top and bottom are designed to go perfectly together.

o **Polished Look:** The matching elements create a deliberate, put-together aesthetic.

o **Versatility (Separates):** The magic lies in their ability to be broken apart. The top can be worn with different bottoms, and vice versa, significantly expanding your wardrobe options.

● **1.4.2 Types of Casual Co-ord Sets:**

o **Top & Pant Sets:** Ranging from relaxed loungewear styles (wide-leg pants with boxy tops) to more tailored, structured casual sets (straight pants with smart tunics or shirts).

o **Top & Skirt Sets:** Often feature a crop top or fitted top with a matching midi or maxi skirt. Can be playful or sophisticated depending on the fabric and print.

o **Shirt & Short Sets:** Ideal for summer, offering a cool and stylish casual look.

● **1.4.3 Styling Your Casual Co-ord Set:**

o **As a Set:** Wear it as designed for an instant, polished look. Add simple accessories like a crossbody bag and sneakers or comfortable flats.

o **Breaking Apart the Set:**

□ **Top with Jeans:** Pair the co-ord top with your favorite jeans for a new casual outfit.

□ **Bottom with Basic Top:** Wear the co-ord pants or skirt with a plain t-shirt, tank top, or a simple kurti for a fresh look.

□ **Layering:** Throw a denim jacket over a co-ord set, or wear the top open over a basic camisole.

1.5 The Art of Elevation: Accessories, Layering, and Footwear
Even the most basic casual outfit can be elevated with smart styling choices. These elements are where your personal touch truly comes into play.
- **1.5.1 The Impact of Accessories:**
o **Scarves & Bandanas:** A printed silk scarf tied around your neck, in your hair, or on your bag can add a pop of color and sophistication.
o **Belts:** Cinch a loose-fitting kurti, a casual dress, or a t-shirt over jeans to define your waist and add structure.
o **Jewellery:**
□ **Minimalist:** Delicate necklaces, stud earrings, simple rings for an understated chic.
□ **Bohemian:** Layered necklaces, stacked bracelets, and larger, earthy earrings.
□ **Ethnic Twist:** A pair of silver jhumkas or a chunky oxidised ring can instantly elevate a simple cotton kurti.
o **Bags:**
□ **Crossbody Bags:** Practical and stylish for hands-free movement.
□ **Tote Bags:** Functional for carrying essentials, choose one in a good quality material.
□ **Stylish Backpacks:** A modern and comfortable alternative for a casual urban look.
- **1.5.2 Mastering Casual Layering:**
o **Denim Jackets:** A timeless classic that pairs with almost anything – jeans, dresses, kurtis, co-ord sets.
o **Light Cardigans/Shrugs:** Perfect for transitional weather or adding a soft layer over sleeveless tops.
o **Kimono Jackets:** Add a bohemian flair and visual interest over a simple top and bottom.
o **Open Shirts:** Wear a plaid or denim shirt open over a basic t-shirt for a relaxed, layered look.

● 1.5.3 Footwear Finesse:
○ **Stylish Sneakers:** The ultimate in comfortable casual chic. Opt for clean, minimalist designs or trendy chunky soles.
○ **Comfortable Sandals/Flats:** Leather sandals, espadrilles, or embellished flats are perfect for warm weather.
○ **Loafers/Mules:** Offer a slightly more polished casual vibe, great for a step up from sneakers.
○ **Juttis/Kolhapuris:** Essential for complementing your casual kurtis and ethnic bottom wear, adding an authentic Indian touch.
○ **Mixfabric's Footwear Pairing Tips:** Consider the overall color palette and the formality of your casual outfit. A printed kurti with matching juttis can be as chic as a monochrome co-ord with white sneakers.

1.6 Building Your Casual Wardrobe Checklist (Actionable)
To help you curate your casual essentials, here's a checklist. Remember to adapt it to your personal needs and preferences.
● Tops:
○ 3-4 quality basic T-shirts (white, black, neutral + 1 accent)
○ 2-3 versatile casual Kurtis (cotton/rayon, different lengths/cuts)
○ 1-2 stylish casual Co-ord Sets
○ 1-2 comfortable casual blouses/shirts
● Bottoms:
○ 2-3 pairs of well-fitting Jeans (different washes/cuts)
○ 1-2 pairs of comfortable Palazzos (for kurtis)
○ 1 pair of versatile Trousers (chinos/linen/relaxed fit)
○ 1 pair of leggings/jeggings (for kurtis)
● Outerwear:
○ 1 Denim Jacket
○ 1 light cardigan/shrug
● Outerwear:
○ 1 Denim Jacket
○ 1 light cardigan/shrug
● Accessories:

Mixfabric Style Tip: Your casual wardrobe is the foundation of your style. By thoughtfully selecting comfortable, versatile, and chic pieces, you empower yourself to face each day with confidence, knowing you look effortlessly put-together. This groundwork allows you to explore the more formal and celebratory aspects of fashion with ease, as we will delve into in the following chapters.

Chapter 2; Power Dressing: For the Office & Beyond

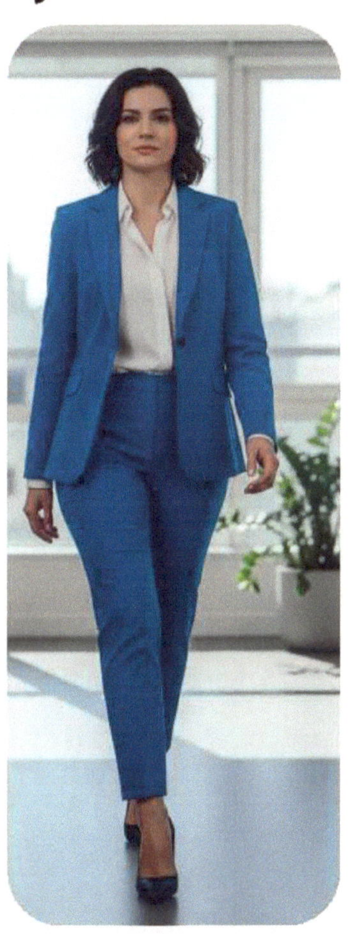

In the competitive landscape of the modern professional world, your attire is often your first ompression. It's a non-verbal résumé that speaks volumes about your attention to detail, professionalism, and confidence. Power dressing isn't about conforming to rigid stereotypes; it's about strategically choosing garments that empower you, convey competence, and allow you to thrive in your workplace. This chapter will equip you with the knowledge to build a powerful and versatile professional wardrobe, one that effortlessly transitions from the boardroom to after-work engagements.

2.1 The Essence of Professional Elegance: Beyond the Dress Code

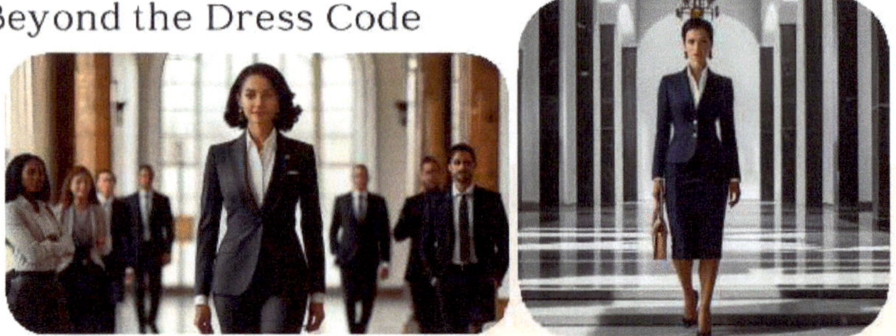

True professional elegance transcends mere adherence to a dress code. It's an art form that blends authority with approachability, and tradition with contemporary flair.

- **Projecting Confidence and Credibility:** Your clothing can subtly influence how you're perceived. Well-fitting, appropriate attire signals that you are meticulous, respectful of the environment, and take your role seriously. This, in turn, boosts your self-assurance.
- **Understanding Your Workplace Culture:** The definition of "professional" varies widely. A creative agency might embrace smart casual, while a corporate law firm demands a more formal approach. Before investing heavily, observe your colleagues, understand unwritten rules, and consider the industry standards.

- **The Intersection of Comfort and Poise:** While looking polished is essential, comfort is equally critical. Clothes that are too tight, restrictive, or made from itchy fabrics will distract you and hinder your focus. When you're physically comfortable, your posture improves, and you exude natural poise.
- **Mixfabric's Vision for Professional Wear:** Mixfabric, advice professional wear that respects traditional aesthetics while integrating modern comfort and versatility. Our fabrics are chosen for their elegant drape, durability, and minimal creasing, ensuring you look sharp throughout your demanding day.

2.2 Core Components of a Polished Professional Wardrobe

- **2.2.1 The Indispensable Blazer:**
○ **The Foundation:** A well-tailored blazer is the cornerstone of professional attire. It instantly pulls an outfit together, adding structure and authority.
○ **Fabric Choices:**
□ **Wool Blends:** Excellent for cooler climates, offering warmth and a crisp drape.
□ **Crepe:** Lightweight, wrinkle-resistant, and drapes beautifully, ideal for warmer climates or travel.
□ **Linen Blends:** Breathable and comfortable for hot weather, offering a relaxed yet refined look.
□ **Cotton Blends:** Versatile and comfortable for everyday wear.
○ **Essential Colors:** Start with black, navy, and charcoal grey. These are incredibly versatile and form the basis of a strong professional capsule.

Building a robust professional wardrobe starts with timeless, versatile pieces that can be mixed and matched to create numerous outfits.

○ **Beyond Neutrals:** Consider adding a blazer in a subtle check, pinstripe, or a rich jewel tone (e.g., emerald green, deep burgundy) to add personality without sacrificing professionalism.
○ **Fit is King:** The shoulders should fit precisely, sleeves should hit at the wrist bone, and the length should be appropriate for your height and style (typically hip-length or slightly longer).

● **2.2.2 Trousers: The Foundation of Your Lower Half:**

○ **Tailored Trousers:** Invest in at least two to three pairs of perfectly fitted tailored trousers.

◻ **Straight-Leg:** A classic, universally flattering cut that creates a clean, streamlined silhouette.

◻ **Slim-Fit/Cigarette Pants:** Modern and sleek, ideal for pairing with longer tunics or kurtis, as well as blazers.

◻ **Wide-Leg/Palazzo Trousers:** Offer a sophisticated, flowing silhouette. When chosen in formal fabrics and tailored lengths, they exude power and elegance, especially flattering for a taller frame.

○ **Fabric and Drape:** Look for fabrics with a good drape that resist creasing, such as crepe, poly-viscose blends, suiting fabrics, or even structured cottons.

○ **Color Matching:** Ensure your trousers complement your blazers and tops. Neutrals like black, navy, grey, and beige are essential.

● **2.2.3 Formal Skirts: Versatility and Femininity:**

○ **Pencil Skirt:** The epitome of office chic. It's figure-hugging but should allow for comfortable movement. Ensure the length is professional (knee-length or just below).

○ **A-line Skirt:** Universally flattering, providing a comfortable fit through the hips and flaring gently towards the hem. Offers a more relaxed formal look.

○ **Midi Skirt (Tailored):** A trendy and sophisticated choice, often in pleated or structured designs, falling to mid-calf.

○ **Fabric Considerations:** Choose fabrics that hold their shape well, such as crepe, structured cotton, wool blends, or even elegant knits.

● **2.2.4 Blouses and Shirts: The Top Layer of Professionalism:**

○ **Classic Button-Down Shirts:** Essential in crisp cotton or silk blends. White, light blue, and subtle stripes are timeless.

○ **Elegant Blouses:** Look for blouses in fabrics like silk, satin, or georgette that offer a soft drape. Consider necklines like boat neck, pussy-bow, or cowl neck.

○ **Shell Tops/Camisoles:** Versatile for layering under blazers or sheer blouses. Opt for quality fabrics that won't pill.

○ **Color & Print:** While solids are safest, subtle prints like polka dots, small florals, or abstract patterns can add personality.

2.3 Integrating Indian Ethnic Wear: A Modern Professional Approach

The modern Indian workplace increasingly embraces ethnic wear, provided it's styled with professionalism and elegance.

- **2.3.1 Structured Kurtis for the Office:**
o **Beyond Casual:** Not all kurtis are suitable for the office. Focus on structured, well-tailored kurtis that exude sophistication.
o **Fabric Choices:** Prioritize cotton silk, linen, crepe, chanderi, or sophisticated
rayon blends. Avoid overly casual cottons, sheer fabrics, or heavily embroidered/embellished festive kurtis for daily office wear.
o **Cuts and Silhouettes:**
□ **Straight Cut Kurtis:** The most professional choice, offering clean lines. Pair with cigarette pants, tailored trousers, or straight palazzos.
□ **A-line Kurtis:** Can be suitable if the flare is subtle and the fabric is formal.
□ **Shirt-Style Kurtis:** Often come with collars and button-down fronts, making
them inherently more formal.
o **Sleeve Length:** Full sleeves or three-quarter sleeves are generally preferred for professional settings.
o **Necklines:** Opt for modest necklines like boat necks, round necks, or collared designs.
o **Embellishments:** Minimalistic and sophisticated. Think subtle thread work, delicate self-embroidery, or discreet buttons. Avoid loud prints, heavy sequins, or excessive glitter.

● 2.3.2 Professional Co-ord Sets with an Indian Touch:

o **The Modern Solution:** Matching sets offer a sophisticated and easy-to-style option for the workplace.

o **Formal Fabrics:** Look for sets in crepe, cotton blends, or subtly textured silk blends.

o **Designs:** Can include well-tailored pant-and-tunic sets, or even a structured short jacket with matching straight trousers.

o **Prints:** Subtle geometric prints, abstract patterns, or muted ethnic motifs can work well. Avoid overly bright or busy prints.

o **Versatility:** The individual pieces can be worn separately – pair the top with formal trousers, or the bottom with a crisp white shirt.

2.4 Fabric Finesse & The Art of Tailoring

The difference between an ordinary outfit and a truly powerful one often lies in the quality of its fabric and the precision of its fit

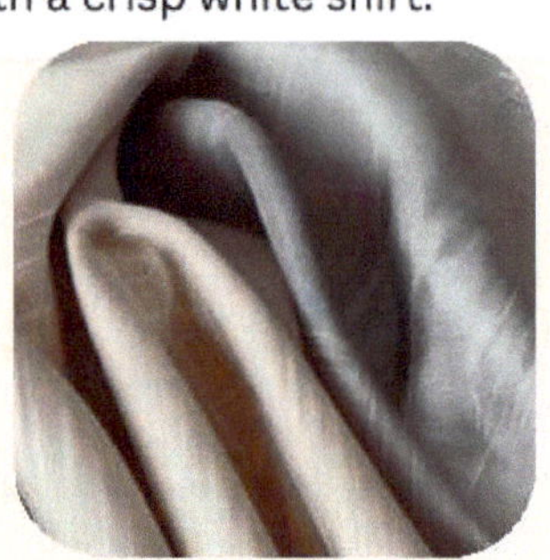

● 2.4.1 Premium Fabric Choices for Professionalism:

o **Cotton (Structured):** For dreathability and crispness. Look for blends or weaves that resist excessive wrinkling.

o **Linen Blends:** Offer the breathability of linen with reduced creasing. Ideal for smart casual or warmer office environments.

o **Crepe:** Drapes beautifully, has a subtle texture, and is largely wrinkle-resistant, making it perfect for blouses, trousers, and light blazers.

o **Viscose/Rayon Blends:** Provide a soft, luxurious feel and excellent drape, often used for elegant blouses and flowy trousers.

o **Silk (Raw Silk, Dupion Silk):** For high-level meetings or formal office events, silk offers unmatched elegance and a rich sheen.

o **Polyester Blends (High Quality):** Modern synthetic blends can offer excellent drape, wrinkle resistance, and durability. Ensure they feel substantial and breathable.

● **2.4.2 The Non-Negotiable: Impeccable Tailoring:**

○ **The Perfect Fit:** Clothing should skim your body, not cling or sag. Shoulders, waist, and length are critical.

○ **Sleeve Length:** Blazer sleeves should end at the wrist bone. Kurti sleeves should be proportional.

○ **Pant Hem:** Trousers should just graze the top of your shoes, with a slight break. Palazzos should almost touch the floor, covering your shoe slightly.

○ **No Gaping or Pulling:** Buttons shouldn't pull, and seams shouldn't strain.

○ **Investment in Alterations:** Even off-the-rack garments can look custom-made with minor alterations. Consider this an essential part of your clothing budget.

2.5 From Desk to Dinner: Seamless Transitions

The modern professional often needs her wardrobe to work overtime, transitioning from a day at the office to an evening event without a full wardrobe change.

● **Strategic Accessorizing:**

○ **Jewellery Swap:** Trade delicate office studs for a bold necklace or statement earrings.

○ **Scarf/Shawl:** A silk scarf can add immediate glamour. Drape it elegantly over your shoulders or tie it around your neck.

○ **Belt:** Add an embellished or metallic belt to cinch a dress or tunic.

- **Footwear Transformation:**
  - **Heels:** Swap comfortable flats or block heels for elegant stilettos or strappy heels to instantly elevate your look.
  - **Metallic/Embellished Shoes:** A pair of shiny or embellished shoes can quickly make an outfit party-ready.
- **Makeup Refresh:**
  - **Lip Color:** A brighter or deeper lip color can instantly transform your face.
  - **Eye Makeup:** A quick swipe of eyeliner or a touch of shimmer can enhance your eyes.
- **Bag Change:** Exchange your professional tote for a chic clutch or a compact evening bag.
- **Outerwear Update:** A structured blazer can be swapped for a stylish leather jacket or a fancy stole.

Mixfabric Style Tip: "When building your professional wardrobe, think of versatile pieces that can be dressed up or down with smart accessories. Our impeccably tailored pant suits and elegant kurtis are designed to offer this seamless transition, ensuring you're ready for anything your day—or evening—brings." By focusing on quality fabrics, impeccable fit, and strategic accessorizing, you can cultivate a professional wardrobe that not only commands respect but also truly reflects your individual style and ambition. Your powerful presence begins with how you present yourself, and with these guidelines, you're well on your way to mastering it.

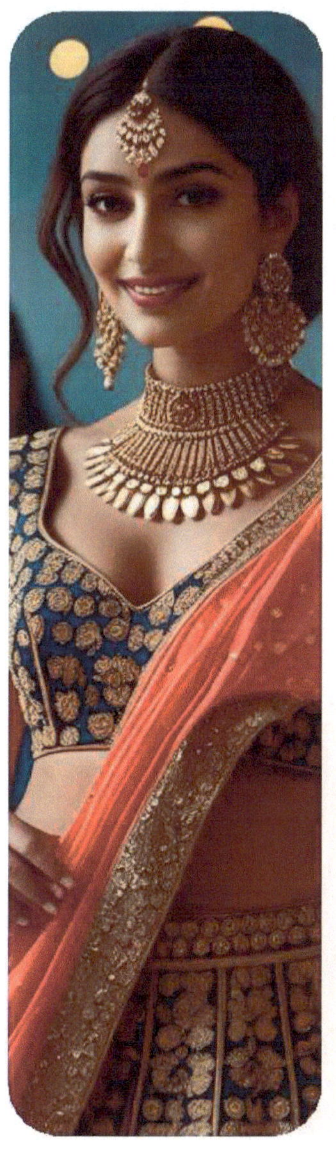# Chapter 3; Party Ready: Glamour for Every Celebration

Life is a series of celebrations, and each occasion calls for an outfit that not only looks stunning but also makes you feel like the life of the party. Party dressing is an art form – a chance to express your most glamorous self, experiment with bolder styles, and embrace shimmer, intricate designs, and luxurious fabrics. This chapter is your ultimate guide to mastering party wear, ensuring you make a memorable entrance and exude confidence at every festive gathering, from intimate soirees to grand receptions.

3.1 The Allure of Celebration: Making a Memorable Entrance

Party wear is inherently about making a statement. It's an opportunity to step out of your everyday comfort zone and embrace exuberance, elegance, or playful glamour.

● **Understanding the Event Vibe:** The first rule of party dressing is to assess the occasion. Is it a casual get-together, a semi-formal cocktail party, a black-tie gala, or a vibrant Indian festival? The formality, venue, and time of day (day vs. evening) will dictate your choices.

● **Confidence as Your Best Accessory:** No matter how stunning your outfit, it's your confidence that truly makes it shine. Choose garments that make you feel incredible, allowing you to move freely, mingle, and enjoy the celebration without discomfort.

● **Balancing Boldness and Elegance:** While parties encourage experimentation, a touch of elegance ensures your look remains sophisticated. This means choosing quality fabrics, well-fitting silhouettes, and strategically placed embellishments.

● **Mixfabric's tips for Party Wear:** We understand that every celebration is unique. Party wear collections are designed to offer a spectrum of styles, from understated elegance to show-stopping glamour, crafted with premium fabrics and exquisite detailing to ensure you shine.

3.2 Party Dresses: Silhouettes for Every Celebration

Dresses are the quintessential party garment, offering a complete and often striking look in one piece. The variety of silhouettes allows for versatility across different event types and body shapes.

● **3.2.1 Sleek & Sophisticated Silhouettes:**

○ **Bodycon/Sheath Dresses:** These dresses hug the body's contours, creating a sleek and confident silhouette.

□ **Best for:** Cocktail parties, club nights, or any event where you want to make a bold, modern statement.

□ **Fabrics:** Often in stretch fabrics like ponte, jersey, or stretch crepe, often with subtle texture or shimmer.

□ **Styling:** Pair with minimalist heels and statement jewellery for a powerful look.

o **Slip Dresses:** Characterized by their minimalist, lingerie-inspired design, usually with spaghetti straps and a fluid, bias-cut drape.

□ **Best for:** Semi-formal dinners, sophisticated evenings, or as a layering piece.

□ **Fabrics:** Satin, silk, or high-quality polyester blends that mimic silk.

□ **Styling:** Can be worn on its own with delicate jewellery, or layered over a slim-fit turtleneck or under a blazer for a chic, contemporary look.

● **3.2.2 Flowy & Feminine Designs:**

o **A-line/Fit-and-Flare Dresses:** Fitted at the bodice and waist, then flaring out gracefully to the hem. Universally flattering as they cinch the waist and skim over hips.

□ **Best for:** Engagement parties, semi-formal gatherings, daytime celebrations, or when you desire a playful yet elegant vibe.

□ **Fabrics:** Chiffon, georgette, structured cotton, or even lighter silks.

□ **Styling:** Can be dressed up with heels and sparkling jewellery or dressed down with elegant flats.

o **Wrap Dresses:** Feature a front closure formed by wrapping one side of the dress over the other, tying at the waist. Incredibly flattering and adjustable.

□ **Best for:** Versatile for almost any party, from casual brunches to evening dinners.

□ **Fabrics:** Jersey, silk, satin, or even crepe.

□ **Styling:** Adaptable with different necklines (V-neck is common) and sleeve lengths, perfect for accentuating the waist.

o **Tiered/Ruffled Dresses:** Incorporate multiple layers or ruffles, adding volume, movement, and a whimsical touch.

□ **Best for:** Festive occasions, garden parties, or when you want a fun, romantic aesthetic.

□ **Fabrics:** Chiffon, organza, or lightweight cottons, often with playful prints.

● **3.2.3 Fabrics and Embellishments for Dresses:**

o **Luxurious Fabrics:**

□ **Satin & Silk:** Offer a lustrous sheen and beautiful drape, perfect for elegant evening wear.

□ **Velvet:** Rich, opulent, and tactile, ideal for winter parties or a regal look.

□ **Lace:** Adds intricate texture, romance, and sophistication.

▢ **Net/Organza:** Sheer and ethereal, often used for overlays, ruffles, or structured elements.

o **Dazzling Embellishments:**

▢ **Sequins:** The ultimate in sparkle, ranging from full-on sequined dresses to subtle sequin accents.

▢ **Beadwork:** Delicate glass or metallic beads sewn onto fabric for intricate patterns.

▢ **Embroidery:** Intricate thread work, sometimes with Zari or Resham, adding traditional or contemporary motifs.

▢ **Cut-Outs & Draping:** Strategically placed cut-outs or artful draping can add a modern, edgy touch.

3.3 Gowns: Red Carpet Ready for Grand Occasions

For the most formal parties, receptions, galas, or black-tie events, a gown is the ultimate choice for grandeur and timeless elegance. Gowns command attention and create a truly magnificent presence.

● **3.3.1 Defining Grandeur: Types of Gowns:**

o **Ball Gowns:** Characterized by a fitted bodice and a dramatically full, voluminous skirt. Creates a fairytale or princess-like silhouette.

▢ **Best for:** High-profile galas, formal receptions, or grand events where maximal impact is desired.

▢ **Fabrics:** Tulle, organza, satin, or heavy silk, often with multiple layers.

o **Mermaid/Trumpet Gowns:** Fitted closely through the bodice, waist, and hips, then flaring out dramatically at or below the knee, resembling a mermaid's tail.

▢ **Best for:** Showcasing curves and creating a glamorous, sophisticated silhouette. Perfect for red-carpet events or lavish receptions.

▢ **Fabrics:** Stretch crepe, satin, or lace, often with intricate embellishments.

o **A-line Gowns:** Fitted bodice and a skirt that gently flares out from the natural waist, forming an "A" shape. Universally flattering and comfortable.

▢ **Best for:** Formal dinners, elegant receptions, or bridesmaid dresses.

▢ **Fabrics:** Chiffon, georgette, silk, or crepe, often with soft drapes.

o **Sheath/Column Gowns:** Straight, form-fitting gowns that skim the body's silhouette from top to bottom.

□ **Best for:** A minimalist, sleek, and sophisticated look. Can be incredibly elegant if impeccably tailored.

□ **Fabrics:** Satin, silk, heavy crepe, often with subtle stretch.

● **3.3.2 Bridal Gowns in Indian Context:**

o While traditionally Western, gowns have become incredibly popular for Indian cocktail parties, receptions, or sangeet ceremonies.

o **Fusion Elements:** Many Mixfabric gowns seamlessly blend Western silhouettes with Indian aesthetics. This can include:

□ **Indian Embellishments:** Zardosi, Resham, beadwork, or mirror work on a Western cut.

□ **Rich Indian Fabrics:** Using silk, velvet, or brocade for a gown.

□ **Attached Dupattas/Capes:** Incorporating a flowing cape or a draped dupatta-like element.

3.4 Co-ord Sets: The Modern Party Game-Changer

Beyond casual, co-ord sets have firmly established themselves as a chic and contemporary choice for parties. They offer a stylish, put-together look with a modern edge.

● **3.4.1 Why Party Co-ords?**

o **Instant Style:** The matching pieces create an immediate, cohesive, and fashion-forward ensemble.

o **Effortless Glamour:** They take the guesswork out of styling, allowing you to focus on accessories.

o **Trendy Appeal:** Co-ords often reflect the latest fashion trends in terms of cuts, prints, and fabrics.

o **Mixfabric's Versatile Co-ords:** Party-ready co-ords that can be dressed up with statement jewellery and heels, or broken apart and styled with other pieces for semi-formal events.

● **3.4.2 Types of Party Co-ord Sets:**

o **Tailored Pant & Top Sets:** Can range from sleek wide-leg pants with a matching fitted top to structured cigarette pants with a peplum or asymmetric top.

o **Skirt & Top Sets:** A popular choice, featuring a matching crop top or fitted blouse with a midi or maxi skirt. The skirt can be A-line, pleated, or even bodycon.

o **Blazer & Short/Pant Sets:** For a chic, fashion-forward look, particularly if the fabric is luxurious (e.g., velvet, sequin).

● **3.4.3 Fabrics & Embellishments for Party Co-ords:**

o **Luxurious Fabrics:** Silk, satin, velvet, brocade, lurex (metallic thread fabric), high-quality crepe.

o **Dazzling Details:** All-over sequins, intricate embroidery (thread, Zari), beadwork, feather detailing, or bold prints (e.g., abstract, maximalist florals).

o **Consider the Cut:** Wide-leg pants with a crop top offer a comfortable yet glamorous vibe. A well-tailored blazer with matching trousers can be incredibly powerful.

3.5 The Grand Finale: Accessorizing for Impact

Accessories are not just additions; they are transformative elements that complete your party look and add that essential sparkle.

● **3.5.1 Jewellery: From Subtle Sparkle to Statement Pieces:**

o **Statement Necklaces:** A bold necklace can transform a simple dress or a plain top, drawing attention to your décolletage.

o **Chandelier Earrings/Jhumkas:** Frame the face beautifully and add immediate glamour, especially if your hair is up or pulled back.

o **Cocktail Rings:** A single, large, dazzling ring can make a significant impact.

o **Cuff Bracelets:** Add a touch of edgy sophistication to sleeveless outfits.

o **Traditional for Ethnic Parties:** Kundan, Polki, Meenakari, or Temple Jewellery sets are essential for Indian weddings and festive parties, perfectly complementing lehengas, gowns, and ethnic suits.

● **3.5.2 Clutches, Bags & Footwear: Completing the Ensemble:**

o **Clutches/Evening Bags:** An absolute must for parties. Choose small, elegant designs that are embellished, metallic, beaded, or feature unique textures. A potli bag is a charming traditional alternative for ethnic parties.

○ **Heels:**

☐ Stilettos: The ultimate in elegance and height, perfect for bodycon dresses, sleek gowns, and tailored pants.

☐ **Block Heels:** Offer more stability and comfort without sacrificing height, great for dancing

☐ **Strappy Heels:** Delicate and feminine, ideal for showcasing well-manicured feet.

☐ **Embellished Pumps/Sandals:** Add a touch of sparkle directly to your feet.

○ **Comfort is Key (But Don't Compromise Style):** If you plan to dance all night, consider block heels or carrying comfortable flats to change into later.

● **3.5.3 Hair & Makeup: The Finishing Touches:**

○ **Hair:**

☐ **Updos:** Elegant and sophisticated (e.g., chignons, sleek buns, braided updos) for formal events, especially with high necklines or intricate backs.

☐ **Glamorous Waves/Curls:** Soft waves or bouncy curls add a touch of romance and volume.

☐ **Sleek & Straight:** For a modern, sharp look.

○ **Makeup:**

☐ **Smoky Eyes:** A classic party look for dramatic flair.

☐ **Bold Lips:** A vibrant red, deep berry, or rich plum can make a strong statement.

☐ **Highlight & Contour:** To define features and add a luminous glow.

☐ **Consider the Outfit:** If your outfit is very intricate, keep makeup a bit more subdued. If the outfit is simple, your makeup can be bolder.

3.6 Preparing for Your Party: A Checklist

To ensure you're fully prepared and fabulous for any celebration:

● **Understand the Dress Code:** Formal, semi-formal, cocktail, festive ethnic, black-tie?

● **Consider the Venue & Time:** Indoor/outdoor, day/night.

● **Comfort Test:** Can you move, sit, and dance comfortably in your chosen outfit and shoes?

- **Accessories Check:** Jewellery, bag, and shoes complement the outfit and occasion.
- **Hair & Makeup Plan:** Decide on your look in advance.
- **Emergency Kit:** A small clutch with lipstick, blotting paper, safety pins, and pain relievers.

Mixfabric Style Tip: "At Mixfabric, we believe glamour isn't just about sparkle; it's about impeccable fit and exquisite craftsmanship. Party dresses, gowns, and co-ord sets are designed to flatter your form and make you feel utterly confident, so you can truly enjoy every moment of your celebration." With these comprehensive guidelines, you are now equipped to confidently navigate the exciting world of party wear. Go forth, embrace the glamour, and make every celebration truly unforgettable!

Chapter 4; The Heart of India: Ethnic Wear Essentials

Indian ethnic wear is more than just clothing; it is a vibrant narrative woven through centuries of cultural heritage, artistic craftsmanship, and evolving traditions. Each stitch, print, and silhouette tells a story reflecting the diverse regions, rituals, and aesthetics of India. This chapter invites you on a profound journey into the heart of Indian fashion, guiding you through its essential categories, understanding their unique characteristics, and showing you how to infuse them with your personal modern style.

4.1 The Timeless Allure of Indian Ethnic Wear:

Tradition Meets Trend Indian fashion has an unparalleled ability to honor its roots while constantly reinventing itself. It's a dynamic interplay between deeply cherished traditions and contemporary global trends.

● **A Tapestry of Culture and Art:** Every piece of traditional Indian attire carries the legacy of generations of artisans, textile techniques, and design philosophies. From intricate embroidery to vibrant block prints, each element contributes to its unique charm.

● **Beyond Occasion-Specific:** While some ethnic garments are reserved for grand celebrations, many, like the versatile kurti or the comfortable palazzo suit, have seamlessly integrated into everyday wardrobes, offering comfort, elegance, and cultural connection.

● **The Power of Personal Expression:** The beauty of Indian ethnic wear lies in its adaptability. It allows for immense personal expression, whether through your choice of fabric, print, silhouette, or the way you accessorize.

● **Mixfabric's Dedication to Heritage:** At Mixfabric, we are deeply rooted in the rich traditions of Indian craftsmanship. We meticulously select fabrics, partner with skilled artisans, and infuse contemporary designs, quality, authenticity, and modern elegance.

4.2 Suits Reimagined: The Diverse World of Salwar Kameez
The term "suit" in Indian fashion predominantly refers to the Salwar Kameez, a versatile three-piece ensemble comprising a kameez (tunic/top), a salwar (bottom), and a dupatta (scarf/stole). The variations in the bottom wear and the kameez cut offer an astonishing range of styles, adapting to every occasion and body type.

● **4.2.1 The Classic & Contemporary:** Pant Suits
○ **Description:** This style features a kameez (tunic) paired with straight-cut, slim-fit, or cigarette-style trousers. The kameez can range from short (hip-length) to long (calf-length), often with side slits for ease of movement.
○ **Vibe:** Offers a sleek, structured, and modern silhouette. It's known for its clean lines and sophisticated appeal.
○ **Best For:** Office wear, business casual, semi-formal gatherings, daily wear, and even travel due to its comfort and ease of movement.
○ **Fabric Choices:** Cotton, linen, rayon, silk blend, crepe, and georgette are popular choices. Structured fabrics hold the silhouette better for formal settings, while softer ones offer comfortable elegance.
○ **Styling Tips:**
□ **For Office:** Pair a solid or subtly printed straight kurti with tailored pants.

● **4.2.2 Flowing Grace:** Palazzo Suits
○ **Description:** Characterized by a kameez (which can be short, knee-length, or long, even Anarkali style) paired with wide-legged palazzo pants. The palazzos are designed to be loose and flowing, offering a comfortable and elegant drape.
○ **Vibe:** Exudes comfort, effortless grace, and a bohemian-chic aesthetic. It's known for its fluid movement and airy feel.
○ **Best For:** Summer wear, festive occasions, casual brunches, garden parties, or whenever you desire a relaxed yet sophisticated look.
○ **Fabric Choices:** Georgette, chiffon, rayon, cotton, linen, and silk blends are common, chosen for their beautiful drape and breathability.

○ **Styling Tips:**

■ **For Everyday:** A printed cotton kurti with a matching or contrasting solid palazzo.

■ **For Festive:** An embellished Anarkali-style kurti with silk palazzos, statement earrings, and a rich dupatta.

■ **For Fusion:** Pair a printed palazzo with a plain Western top and a denim jacket.

● **4.2.3 Playful & Festive: Sharara Suits**

○ **Description:** Feature a short or knee-length kameez paired with sharara pants, which are fitted at the waist and flare dramatically from the knee downwards, resembling a skirt. The flare is often achieved through gathers, pleats, or multiple tiers.

○ **Vibe:** Inherently festive, vibrant, and playful. They hark back to Mughal-era fashion and are known for their lively movement and celebratory feel.

○ **Best For:** Weddings, sangeets, mehndi ceremonies, festive gatherings, and special occasions.

○ **Fabric Choices:** Silk, velvet, georgette, net, often heavily embroidered with zari, sequin, mirror work, or intricate thread work.

○ **Styling Tips:** Pair with traditional jewellery like jhumkas, a maang tikka, and bangles. Opt for embellished juttis or block heels.

● **4.2.4 Traditional Charm: Garara Suits**

○ **Description:** Similar to shararas, garara pants also have a wide flare, but the key distinction is that the flare starts much higher, typically at or above the knee, and is often accentuated by a ruched or gathered band at the knee. This creates a distinct, layered look.

○ **Vibe:** Often considered more traditional and historically rich than shararas, offering a distinct aristocratic charm.

○ **Best For:** Formal ethnic events, traditional weddings, and occasions where a regal, classic look is desired.

○ **Fabric Choices & Embellishments:** Similar to shararas, they are often seen in silks, velvets, or brocades, adorned with elaborate Zardosi, Resham, or Gota Patti work.

○ **Styling Tips:** Best complemented with heavy traditional jewellery and classic hairstyles.

● **4.2.5 Fusion & Flair: Skirt Suits**

○ **Description:** This style combines a long kurti or a shorter kameez (often with a contemporary cut like a peplum or asymmetric hem) with a voluminous or straight ethnic skirt.

○ **Vibe:** A beautiful fusion look, offering the grandeur of a lehenga with the comfort and versatility of a suit. It can be traditional or modern depending on the cut and embellishments.

○ **Best For:** Festive occasions, semi-formal parties, cultural events, or even as an elegant bridesmaid outfit.

○ **Fabric Choices:** Cotton silk, chanderi, georgette, raw silk, often featuring vibrant prints or subtle embroidery on both the top and skirt.

○ **Styling Tips:** This versatile ensemble can be styled with oxidised silver jewellery for a bohemian feel, or traditional gold for a festive look. Experiment with different dupatta drapes or opt for a cape-style top.

4.3 The Versatile Hero: The Kurti

The kurti is arguably the most adaptable and ubiquitous garment in the Indian woman's wardrobe. Its journey from simple daily wear to a staple for festive celebrations is a testament to its unparalleled versatility.

● **4.3.1 In-Depth: Kurti Cuts & Styles:**

○ **Straight Cut:** Offers a lean, elongated silhouette. Best paired with cigarette pants, fitted trousers, or even jeans for a modern, sophisticated look.

○ **A-line:** Fitted at the bust and gently flares out, providing a flattering silhouette for most body types. Comfortable and graceful for daily wear or semi-formal occasions.

○ **Anarkali:** Features a fitted bodice and a voluminous flare starting from the bust or waist, reminiscent of a frock. Ranges from simple daily wear versions in cotton to heavily embellished floor-length pieces for grand events.

○ **High-Low:** Characterized by a shorter front hem and a longer back hem, creating a trendy, asymmetrical appeal.

o **Asymmetric/Diagonal Hem:** Unique, uneven hemlines that add an artistic and modern edge to the kurti.

o **C-Cut/U-Cut Hem:** Hems that are curved upwards at the sides, offering a modern look, often seen in more contemporary designs.

o **Jacket Style/Layered Kurti:** Features an attached or detachable jacket overlay, or distinct layers, adding dimension and a formal touch.

o **Shirt-Style Kurti:** Designed with a collar and button-down front, resembling a long shirt. Can be worn as a tunic, a dress, or an open jacket.

● **4.3.2 The Spectrum of Kurti Fabrics:**

o **Cotton:** The perennial favorite. Offers unmatched breathability, comfort, and ease of maintenance. Varieties include:

□ **Mulmul:** Soft, sheer, and incredibly lightweight, perfect for summer.

□ **Cambric:** Denser weave, more opaque, ideal for structured casual wear.

□ **Rayon Cotton:** A blend offering softness, drape, and breathability.

o **Rayon/Viscose:** Known for its silky texture, beautiful drape, and vibrant color retention. Excellent for elegant casual wear and semi-formal kurtis.

o **Linen:** Highly absorbent and breathable, with a distinct natural texture. Perfect for a sophisticated, relaxed look, especially in warmer climates.

o **Chanderi:** A blend of silk and cotton, known for its sheer texture, lightweight feel, and subtle sheen. Ideal for semi-formal and festive kurtis.

o **Silk (Art Silk, Tussar Silk, Raw Silk, Chiffon Silk):** Offers luxurious sheen, rich texture, and a celebratory feel. Perfect for festive and formal kurtis with embroidery.

o **Georgette & Chiffon:** Sheer, lightweight, and flowing fabrics that offer a graceful drape, often used for layered kurtis or those with extensive embellishments.

o **Velvet:** Rich, soft, and opulent, ideal for winter wear and grand festive occasions, often featuring heavy embroidery.

o **Brocade:** A heavily woven fabric with raised patterns, often in silk, giving a regal and traditional look, perfect for a grand kurti.

● **4.3.3 Elevating Your Kurti: Styling for Every Occasion:**

o **Daily Wear:** A simple cotton kurti with leggings, jeggings, or straight pants. Add comfortable sandals or juttis.

o **Casual Outings/Brunch:** A printed rayon or cotton kurti with comfortable palazzos or culottes. Accessorize with statement earrings and a casual bag.

o **Semi-Formal Gatherings/Small Functions:** A Chanderi or silk-blend kurti with subtle embroidery, paired with cigarette pants or tailored palazzos. Elevate with heels and elegant jewellery.

o **Festive Celebrations:** A heavily embellished Anarkali or straight-cut kurti in silk or georgette, paired with matching churidars or palazzos. Complete the look with a rich dupatta, traditional jewellery, and embellished footwear.

o **Fusion Look:** A short kurti worn over a pair of jeans, or an asymmetric kurti styled with a long ethnic skirt.

4.4 Understanding Fabrics, Embroidery, and Prints: The Soul of Ethnic Wear

The true artistry of Indian ethnic wear lies in its intricate details – the choice of fabric, the narrative told through its prints, and the painstaking beauty of its embroidery.

● **4.4.1 The Language of Fabrics:**

o **Natural Fibers:**

□ **Cotton:** The most widely used. Its comfort and breathability make it ideal for everyday.

□ **Silk:** Encompasses numerous varieties (Banarasi, Kanjeevaram, Tussar, Raw Silk, Mysore Silk), each with unique textures and sheens, used for rich formal wear.

□ **Linen:** Known for its breathability and natural texture, ideal for sophisticated casual and semi-formal wear.

o **Synthetic & Blended Fibers (with natural feel):**

□ **Georgette & Chiffon:** Lightweight, sheer, and flowing, perfect for drapes and ethereal layers.

□ **Crepe:** Drapes beautifully, has a subtle texture, and is largely wrinkle-resistant.

□ **Rayon/Viscose:** Mimics silk, offering a soft feel and excellent drape.

□ **Velvet:** A luxurious, dense piled fabric, perfect for winter festive wear.

□ **Brocade:** A rich, patterned fabric, often woven with metallic threads, giving a royal look.

● **4.4.2 The Art of Embroidery:**

o **Zari/Zardosi:** Intricate, heavy embroidery using gold or silver metallic threads. A hallmark of traditional bridal and formal wear, often incorporating sequins and beads.

o **Resham:** Fine silk thread embroidery, creating delicate floral, abstract, or figurative patterns in a wide range of colors. Offers a softer, more elegant look.

o **Gota Patti:** An appliqué technique from Rajasthan, where small pieces of gold or silver ribbon are sewn onto the fabric to create patterns. Adds subtle shimmer and traditional charm.

o **Mirror Work:** Tiny mirrors (shisha) stitched onto fabric, reflecting light and adding a rustic yet festive sparkle. Popular in Gujarat and Rajasthan.

o **Chikankari:** Delicate, subtle white-on-white (or colored thread on pastel fabric) embroidery from Lucknow, known for its intricate, airy patterns.

o **Phulkari:** A vibrant folk embroidery from Punjab, characterized by dense floral and geometric patterns, often on cotton or silk.

o **Aari Work:** Chain stitch embroidery, often done with a hooked needle, creating intricate, raised patterns.

o **Sequins & Cutdana:** Small, flat, shiny discs (sequins) or tiny cylindrical beads (cutdana) stitched onto fabric to create dazzling effects.

● 4.4.3 The Diversity of Prints:
○ **Block Printing:** A traditional hand-printing technique using carved wooden blocks Famous styles include Bagru, Sanganeri, Dabu, and Ajrakh prints, often featuring geometric, floral, or animal motifs.
○ **Bandhani/Tie-Dye:** A traditional resist-dyeing method where fabric is tied in small knots before dyeing, creating unique patterns like dots, waves, or squares. Vibrant and lively.
○ **Batik:** A wax-resist dyeing technique that creates intricate patterns with a distinct cracked effect.
○ **Screen Printing:** A versatile technique that allows for a wide range of designs and colors, offering both traditional and modern prints.
○ **Digital Printing:** Modern technology allows for highly intricate, photo-realistic, and vibrant designs to be printed onto fabric, offering limitless creative possibilities.

4.5 The Dupatta & Stole: The Soulful Drape
The dupatta (a long scarf or shawl) is an integral and often transformative element of many Indian ethnic ensembles. It adds grace, modesty, and is a canvas for intricate design.
● **Its Role:** From completing a suit to adding an extra layer of elegance, the dupatta offers versatility in styling and enhances the overall look.
● **Fabric & Embellishment:** Dupattas can range from lightweight chiffon and georgette for daily wear to heavy silk, velvet, or net with elaborate embroidery or borders for festive occasions.
● **Styling Techniques:**
○ **Classic Drape:** Over both shoulders, or pinned neatly over one shoulder.
○ **Side Drape:** Draped over one shoulder and brought around to the front.
○ **Neck Wrap:** For a casual, contemporary look, especially with lighter fabrics.
○ **Cape Style:** A heavier, often embellished dupatta can be draped over the shoulders like a cape.

4.6 Footwear & Jewellery: The Finishing Touches for Ethnic Elegance
No ethnic outfit is complete without the perfect pairing of footwear and jewellery, which add authenticity and polish.
● 4.6.1 Ethnic Footwear Essentials:
○ **Juttis/Mojaris:** Traditional handcrafted leather shoes, often embroidered or embellished. They are versatile and comfortable, perfect for almost all ethnic outfits.

o **Kolhapuris:** Handcrafted leather sandals from Maharashtra, known for their unique design and comfort. Ideal for casual and semi-casual ethnic wear.

o **Embellished Heels/Wedges:** For a more formal or taller look, especially with lehengas, gowns, or heavier suits. Look for designs with ethnic embroidery or crystal detailing.

o **Block Heels:** Offer more stability and comfort than stilettos while still providing elevation.

● **4.6.2 The Radiance of Ethnic Jewellery:**

o **Jhumkas:** Bell-shaped earrings, a classic Indian design, suitable for almost all ethnic outfits.

o **Chaandbalis:** Crescent moon-shaped earrings, often intricate and embellished, perfect for festive wear.

o **Maang Tikka:** A head ornament worn on the forehead, typically for formal events and bridal wear.

o **Nath (Nose Ring):** Can range from simple studs to elaborate rings, a significant part of bridal and highly traditional looks.

o **Bangles & Kadas:** Essential for completing the traditional Indian look, worn in sets or as single statement pieces.

o **Kundan/Polki Sets:** Uncut diamond jewellery, highly prized for its traditional, regal look, often paired with elaborate wedding or festive outfits.

o **Meenakari:** Enamel work on metal, creating vibrant, colorful designs, often seen in earrings and necklaces.

o **Temple Jewellery:** Traditional gold jewellery adorned with motifs of gods and goddesses, popular in South India.

o **Oxidised Silver Jewellery:** Offers a rustic, bohemian, and antique look, perfect for a contemporary ethnic style.

o **Mixfabric's Jewellery Pairing Tips:** When selecting jewellery, consider the neckline of your outfit, the type of embroidery, and the overall formality of the occasion. Less is often more with heavily embellished garments.

Mixfabric Style Tip: "Embrace the journey of discovering your ethnic style. Experiment with different silhouettes, fabrics, and accessories to find what truly resonates with your spirit and makes you feel connected to our rich heritage." The world of Indian ethnic wear is endlessly fascinating and rich. By understanding its fundamental elements, you can confidently curate a wardrobe that celebrates your heritage and allows you to shine with grace and authenticity at every occasion.

Chapter 5; Ritual & Celebration: Dressing for Indian Occasions

India is a land of vibrant celebrations, where every season brings forth a tapestry of festivals, ceremonies, and cherished rituals. From the spiritual solemnity of a Puja to the boisterous joy of Diwali, each occasion holds a unique significance and, often, a distinct unwritten dress code. Dressing appropriately for these events is not merely about looking good; it's about showing respect for tradition, embracing cultural heritage, and participating fully in the joyous spirit of the moment. This chapter will be your definitive guide to navigating the diverse world of Indian festive wear, ensuring you always strike the perfect balance between cultural reverence and your personal, modern style.

5.1 The Spirit of Indian Celebrations: Why Attire Matters

In India, clothing is often intertwined with cultural identity, spirituality, and social symbolism. Wearing the right attire for a specific ritual or festival enhances the experience and demonstrates respect.

● **Honoring Tradition:** Many garments, colors, and styles have historical or religious significance. Choosing them appropriately reflects an understanding and appreciation of cultural customs.

● **Embracing the Festive Spirit:** Vibrant colors, intricate embellishments, and flowing silhouettes are often synonymous with celebration. Dressing up amplifies the festive mood for you and those around you.

● **Comfort and Practicality:** While grandeur is key, especially for larger events, comfort is paramount. Long hours of ceremonies, mingling, and often dancing necessitate breathable fabrics and practical designs.

5.2 Dressing for Major Indian Festivals & Occasions: A Detailed Guide

Each festival in India has its own unique charm and, consequently, its preferred style of dress.

● **5.2.1 Diwali & Eid: Grandeur and Radiance**

o **Vibe:** These are two of the most significant and widely celebrated festivals in India, characterized by immense joy, light, family gatherings, feasting, and gift exchanges. They call for grand, celebratory, and often opulent attire.

o and

□ **Heavy Anarkali Suits:** Floor-length Anarkalis with intricate embroidery (Zardosi, Resham, sequin work) on rich fabrics like silk, velvet, or georgette. They offer a regal and graceful silhouette, perfect for grand evening parties or family gatherings.

□ **Sharara/Garara Suits:** Highly popular for their festive flair and traditional roots. Choose sets with heavy embellishments in luxurious fabrics. They offer a playful yet grand look, especially suited for movement and dancing.

◻ **Lighter Lehengas/Half Sarees:** For family gatherings or more intimate festive parties, a relatively lighter lehenga (compared to bridal lehengas) or a half-saree (often with pre-stitched drapes for ease) is a fantastic choice. Look for vibrant colors, mirror work, or Gota Patti.

◻ **Ethnic Gowns (Fusion):** For modern festive parties, an Indo-Western gown

with traditional Indian embroidery or motifs can be a stunning choice, blending global style with Indian heritage.

◻ **Classic Sarees:** Rich silk sarees (Banarasi, Kanjeevaram), or heavily embroidered georgette/net sarees are timeless choices for elegance and tradition.

○ **Color Palette:** Embrace vibrant and auspicious colors like deep reds, emerald greens, royal blues, sunny yellows, fuchsia, gold, and silver. Jewel tones are always a festive favorite.

● 5.2.2 Rakhi & Bhaidooj: Affectionate & Charming

○ **Vibe:** These festivals celebrate sibling bonds, marked by affectionate gatherings, traditional rituals, and often, delicious food. The attire should be comfortable yet charming, reflecting the warmth of family.

○ **Attire Suggestions:**

◻ **Stylish Kurtis with Palazzos/Cigarette Pants:** Opt for kurtis in cotton silk, chanderi, or high-quality rayon with elegant prints, subtle embroidery, or unique cuts. Pair with comfortable palazzos or sleek cigarette pants.

◻ **Simple Anarkali Suits:** A lightweight Anarkali in a soft fabric like cotton or

georgette, with minimal embellishments, offers a touch of grace without being overly formal.

◻ **Ethnic Co-ord Sets:** A printed ethnic top with matching palazzo or a long skirt can be a stylish and cohesive choice.

◻ **Light Sarees:** Cotton silk or georgette sarees with minimal work are comfortable and elegant for these family-centric events.

○ **Color Palette:** Pastels, soft floral prints, pleasant blues, greens, yellows, and pinks. Muted jewel tones can also work.

● **5.2.3 Pujas & Religious Ceremonies: Reverence and Modesty**

o **Vibe:** These occasions are centered around spiritual devotion, prayer, and quiet reverence. The attire should reflect modesty, simplicity, and respect.

o **Attire Suggestions:**

□ **Traditional Salwar Suits:** Opt for classic suits with churidars or straight pants. Fabrics like cotton, silk, or chanderi are ideal. Keep embroidery minimal and elegant.

□ **Simple, Full-Sleeved Kurtis:** Paired with leggings, churidars, or comfortable straight pants. Avoid sleeveless or overly revealing necklines.

□ **Sarees:** Elegant silk sarees (e.g., Banarasi, Kanjeevaram, simple silk), cotton sarees, or traditional printed sarees are timeless and highly respected choices. Ensure the pallu is draped modestly.

□ **Anarkalis (Subtle):** If opting for an Anarkali, choose a solid color or one with very subtle work, ensuring it's not overly flared or embellished.

o **Color Palette:** Often lighter, auspicious colors like white, cream, yellow, saffron, or light pastels. Avoid black or overly flashy colors unless specific to a regional tradition.

● **5.2.4 Other Ceremonies (e.g., Housewarming, Engagements, Baby Showers, Naming Ceremonies):**

o **Vibe:** These events vary widely in formality based on the family's preference and scale. They are usually joyous, social gatherings.

o **Attire Suggestions:**

□ **Elegant Anarkali Suits or Gowns:** For larger, more formal engagements or receptions. Look for tasteful embroidery and refined fabrics

□ **Designer Suits with Modern Cuts:** Pant suits or palazzo suits with contemporary cuts, unique necklines, or subtle fusion elements.

. □ **Indo-Western Fusion Wear:** Such as a stylish kurti paired with a long ethnic skirt, a crop top with a flowing cape, or a pant-saree.

□ **Stylish Sarees:** Designer sarees, pre-draped sarees, or elegant traditional sarees with modern blouses.

○ **Color Palette:** Wide range, from soft pastels to vibrant jewel tones, depending on the time of day and family's preference.

5.3 Balancing Tradition with Personal Style: The Modern Woman's Approach

The beauty of Indian fashion is its flexibility. You don't have to choose between adhering to tradition and expressing your individuality.

● **Modern Cuts, Traditional Fabrics:** Consider a sleek, straight-cut suit crafted from rich Banarasi silk, or a contemporary peplum-style top paired with a traditional ethnic skirt.

● **Traditional Silhouettes, Contemporary Embellishments:** An Anarkali with modern geometric embroidery, or a lehenga featuring minimalist sequin work instead of heavy Zari.

● **Strategic Color Play:** Experiment with unconventional color combinations or pastels for traditionally vibrant occasions. A pastel lehenga for a Mehendi, or a deep emerald suit for a Diwali gathering.

● **Mix & Match Magic:** Pair a traditional Banarasi dupatta with a simple silk kurti and modern cigarette pants. Wear an embroidered ethnic top with a pair of well-fitted jeans for a chic fusion look.

5.4 The Essential Role of Dupattas and Stoles in Indian Rituals

The dupatta is more than just an accessory; it's a vital component of many Indian ethnic ensembles, offering grace, versatility, and often, a symbol of modesty or tradition.

- **Cultural Significance:** In many rituals, covering the head with a dupatta is a sign of respect, especially when entering temples or during religious ceremonies.
- **Transformative Power:** A simple suit can be dramatically elevated by a heavily embroidered, richly textured, or vibrantly printed dupatta.
- Styling for Occasion:
o **Traditional Drape:** Over one shoulder and across the chest, or neatly pleated and pinned over both shoulders. For Pujas or solemn events, it might be draped over the head.
o **Contemporary Drape:** Loosely draped over one arm, wrapped casually around the neck, or even used as a stylish cape over an ethnic gown.

5.5 Completing the Look: Footwear and Jewellery Pairing for Indian Rituals Accessories are the crowning glory of any Indian ethnic outfit, adding the essential sparkle, authenticity, and polish.

- **5.5.1 Footwear for Festivities:**
o **Juttis/Mojaris:** The quintessential choice for almost all ethnic outfits. Opt for embroidered, embellished, or mirrored juttis for festive occasions.
o **Kolhapuris:** A comfortable and stylish traditional sandal, great for casual to
semi-formal ethnic wear.
o **Embellished Block Heels/Wedges:** Provide comfort and height for long events, especially suitable with Anarkalis, Gowns, or heavy suits.
o **Stilettos/Kitten Heels:** For more formal events, especially with designer suits or fusion gowns.

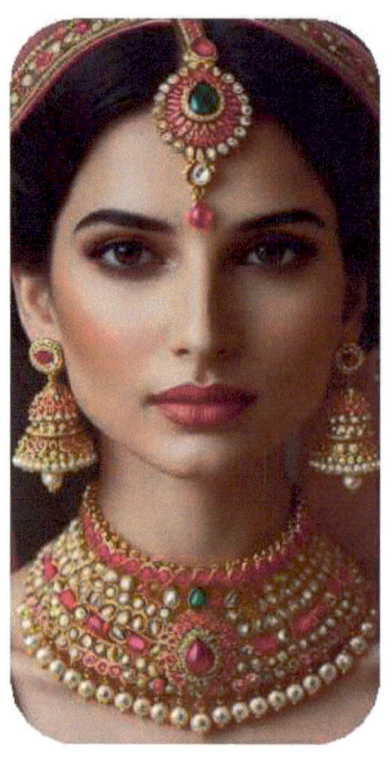

- **5.5.2 Jewellery: The Grandeur of Indian Adornment:**
o **Traditional Sets:** For grand occasions, full sets of Kundan, Polki, Meenakari, or Temple Jewellery are ideal. These typically include a necklace, earrings (jhumkas or chaandbalis), and often a maang tikka.
o **Statement Earrings:** A pair of elaborate jhumkas or large chandbalis can be enough to elevate a simpler outfit.
o **Bangles & Kadas:** Crucial for an authentic Indian look. Layer delicate bangles or opt for a few chunky kadas.
o **Maang Tikka/Passa:** These head adornments add significant traditional flair, especially for grand festive and wedding-related events.
o **Nath (Nose Ring):** For a truly traditional or bridal aesthetic, a classic nose ring can be incredibly striking.

Mixfabric Style Tip: "When dressing for traditional Indian rituals, the essence lies in expressing koy and respect. Don't be afraid to embrace color and rich embellishments, but always consider the specific nuances of the ceremony. Mixfabric's festive guide are curated to help you celebrate every occasion with confidence, comfort, and undeniable style." By understanding the cultural significance and stylistic nuances of Indian festivals and rituals, you can confidently curate an ethnic wardrobe that not only looks stunning but also deeply connects you to the vibrant heart of Indian culture.

Chapter 6; The Bridal Dream: Lehengas, Gowns & More for the Big Day

A wedding is a symphony of emotions, traditions, and unforgettable moments, and for the bride, her attire is the crescendo of her most cherished dream. It's not merely a dress; it's a living canvas of her personality, her heritage, and the beginning of her new journey. But the wedding attire journey extends beyond the bride, encompassing the elegantly dressed bridal party and the tastefully adorned guests. This chapter delves deep into the opulent world of Indian bridal and wedding guest attire, focusing on the majestic lehengas, glamorous gowns, and other exquisite ensembles that define the grand Indian wedding spectacle.

6.1 The Ultimate Bridal Ensemble: Making Your Dream a Reality

For a bride, choosing her wedding outfit is an intensely personal and often emotional experience. It's about finding that perfect blend of beauty, comfort, and symbolic significance.

● **Vision Boarding Your Dream:** Before you even begin shopping, create a vision board. What aesthetic appeals to you? Traditional, contemporary, minimalist, regal, bohemian? What colors, fabrics, and embellishments have you always envisioned for your big day?

● **Understanding Your Body & Comfort:** While grand, your bridal outfit should also be comfortable enough for you to move, sit, and genuinely enjoy your special day. An uncomfortable outfit can detract from your experience. Consider your body shape and choose silhouettes that flatter and make you feel confident.

● **The Significance of Tradition:** Indian bridal wear is steeped in cultural meaning. Red often symbolizes love and prosperity, while certain embroideries carry regional significance. Understanding these elements can add depth to your choice.

6.2 Lehengas: From Traditional Grandeur to Contemporary Pastels

The lehenga choli is the quintessential Indian bridal attire, celebrated for its majestic appeal and versatility. It consists of three key components: the lehenga (the long, pleated skirt), the choli (the fitted blouse), and the dupatta (the long scarf or veil).

● **6.2.1 The Traditional Indian Bridal Lehenga:**

○ **Fabrics of Royalty:**

□ **Silk:** (e.g., Banarasi, Kanjeevaram, Raw Silk, Dupion Silk, Tussar Silk) Offers a rich sheen, luxurious feel, and holds heavy embroidery beautifully. Each type has its unique texture and drape.

□ **Velvet:** Opulent, regal, and ideal for winter weddings, providing a rich depth of color and softness.

□ **Net/Georgette:** Often used as an overlay for a lighter, more ethereal look, allowing intricate embellishments to stand out.

○ **Embellishments That Tell a Story:**

□ **Zardosi/Zari:** Intricate, heavy embroidery using metallic gold or silver threads, often combined with beads, pearls, and semi-precious stones. It creates a rich, raised effect.

☐ **Resham:** Delicate and intricate silk thread embroidery, creating detailed floral, figurative, or abstract patterns. Offers a softer, more refined look.

☐ **Gota Patti:** An appliqué technique from Rajasthan, where small pieces of gold or silver ribbon are sewn onto the fabric to create patterns. Adds a traditional shimmer.

☐ **Dabka/Kundankari:** Raised embroidery using fine springs of metallic thread (dabka) or setting Kundan (glass stones) onto the fabric.

☐ **Sequins & Beadwork:** Adds sparkle and texture, ranging from subtle scattering to dense, all-over embellishment.

○ **Classic Bridal Colors:**

☐ **Reds:** The most traditional and auspicious color, symbolizing love, prosperity, and new beginnings. Shades include vermilion, crimson, maroon, and cherry red.

☐ **Deep Jewel Tones:** Emerald green, royal blue, deep burgundy, and majestic purple are popular alternatives, often chosen for their regal appeal.

○ **Traditional Silhouettes:**

☐ **Circular/Flared Lehenga:** The most voluminous and traditional, creating a grand, swirling effect, perfect for a majestic bridal entry.

☐ **A-line Lehenga:** Fitted at the waist and gently flares out, forming an "A" shape. Universally flattering and offers a balanced look.

☐ **Kalidar Lehenga:** Features multiple vertical panels (kali) sewn together to create a flared skirt, often with contrasting fabrics or embroidery on each panel.

● **6.2.2 The Contemporary Bridal Lehenga:**

○ **Fabrics with a Modern Twist:**

☐ **Organza:** Lightweight, stiff, and sheer, offering a modern, structured yet ethereal look.

☐ **Satin:** Provides a sleek, lustrous finish for a minimalist yet elegant feel.

☐ **Tulle:** Often used for layers to create volume with a delicate, soft appearance.

○ **Subtler Embellishments:**

□ **Delicate Thread Work:** Fine, intricate thread embroidery that focuses on subtle textures and patterns rather than heavy opulence.

□ **Pearls & Crystals:** Used sparingly or in delicate patterns for refined sparkle.

□ **Cutdana & Glass Beads:** For a modern, understated shimmer.

□ **Minimalist Designs:** Focus on the cut, fabric, and drape with minimal, strategically placed embellishments.

○ **The Pastel Revolution:**

□ Blush Pink, Mint Green, Powder Blue, Peach, Lavender: These soft, romantic hues have become incredibly popular, offering a fresh, contemporary alternative to traditional reds.

□ **Ivory & Gold:** A sophisticated and timeless combination for a chic, modern

bridal look.

□ **Dual-Tones/Ombré:** Blending two or more colors seamlessly, adding depth and visual interest.

○ **Modern Silhouettes:**

□ **Mermaid/Trumpet Lehenga:** Fitted closely through the hips and thighs, then flares out dramatically at or below the knee, creating a glamorous, body-hugging silhouette.

□ **Jacket Lehenga:** Features a long, often embellished jacket worn over a simple choli and lehenga, adding a contemporary layer and grandeur.

□ **Peplum Choli Lehenga:** A choli with a flared peplum hem, adding a trendy

and flattering detail.

□ **Lehenga with Trails:** An extended back hem for a dramatic, sweeping effect.

6.3 Bridal Gowns: For Cocktail, Reception, or Fusion Ceremonies

While lehengas hold traditional significance, Western-inspired gowns have become highly sought-after choices for pre-wedding functions like cocktail parties and sangeets, as well as for the grand wedding reception or for brides opting for a fusion ceremony.

- **6.3.1 Popular Bridal Gown Styles:**

o **Ball Gowns:** Voluminous skirts with fitted bodices, creating a dramatic, fairytale effect. Ideal for a grand entrance at a reception.

o **Mermaid Gowns:** Hug the body from the chest to the knee, then flare out dramatically. Emphasize curves and offer a highly glamorous silhouette.

o **A-line Gowns:** Fitted at the bodice and gently flare out, universally flattering and comfortable for long hours.

o **Sheath/Column Gowns:** Straight, form-fitting gowns that skim the body, offering a sleek, minimalist, and sophisticated look.

o **Trail Gowns:** Feature an extended back hem that sweeps behind the bride, adding a dramatic, red-carpet appeal.

- **6.3.2 Fusion of Cultures: Indian Elements in Bridal Gowns:**

o **Embellishments:** Gowns often feature intricate Indian embroidery (Zardosi, Resham, sequin work, crystal embellishments) applied to Western silhouettes, creating a unique fusion.

o **Fabrics:** Luxurious Indian fabrics like raw silk, brocade, or rich velvet can be used to create gowns with a distinct cultural touch.

o **Draping:** Incorporating elements like an attached dupatta-like drape or a flowing cape that mimics a traditional veil.

6.4 Pre-Wedding Rituals: Outfits for Haldi, Mehendi, Sangeet, and Engagement

Each pre-wedding ceremony has its own unique ambiance and dress code, offering the bride and her close ones opportunities to wear different styles and colors.

- **6.4.1 Haldi Ceremony:**

o **Vibe:** Joyful, informal, and vibrant. Involves applying turmeric paste to the bride/groom.

o **Attire:** Simple, comfortable, and often vibrant yellow. A plain yellow cotton kurti-palazzo set, a simple yellow lehenga with minimal work, or a comfortable short Anarkali. The fabric should be washable!

o **Mixfabric's Haldi Picks:** Comfortable and chic yellow ensembles that allow for easy movement and joyful participation.

● **6.4.2 Mehendi Ceremony:**
o **Vibe:** Lively, playful, and often involves dancing and intricate henna application. Comfort and practicality are key while looking festive.
o **Attire:** Sharara suits (comfortable for sitting with henna), light lehengas (A-line or circular in lighter fabrics), skirt-kurti sets, or stylish palazzo suits. Sleeveless or short-sleeved tops are practical for henna application.
o **Color Palette:** Greens, pinks, blues, multi-colors. Floral prints, mirror work, and Gota Patti are popular.
o **Mixfabric's Mehendi Collection:** Vibrant and comfortable outfits with playful designs, perfect for a lively day.
● **6.4.3 Sangeet Ceremony:**
o **Vibe:** High-energy, glamorous, and focused on music, dance, and celebration.
o **Attire:** Can range from heavily embroidered lehengas (less heavy than wedding lehenga), glamorous gowns, designer suits (like a pant suit with a dramatic cape), or contemporary fusion wear. Embellishments like sequins, crystals, and elaborate thread work are popular.
o **Color Palette:** Jewel tones, metallics, deep blues, reds, and fuchsia are popular.
● **6.4.4 Engagement Ceremony:**
o **Vibe:** Semi-formal to formal, marking the official beginning of the wedding festivities.
o **Attire:** Elegant gowns, sophisticated lehengas (often in pastels or contemporary colors), designer suits, or fusion ensembles. The look is usually more refined than Mehendi/Haldi but less heavy than the main wedding day.
6.5 Understanding Cuts, Drapes, and Embellishments for Bridal Wear
The magic of bridal wear is in its intricate details and how they combine to create a cohesivemasterpiece.
● **6.5.1 The Art of the Cut & Silhouette:**
o **Necklines:** Sweetheart, off-shoulder, illusion, deep V, high-neck, boat neck – each creates a different focal point and frames the face.

o **Sleeve Styles:** Cap sleeves, short sleeves, three-quarter sleeves, full sleeves, bishop sleeves, puffed sleeves – impact the overall silhouette and comfort.

o **Back Designs:** Deep backs, sheer backs with embroidery, keyhole backs, Dori (tie-up) backs – add an element of allure.

o **Choli Lengths:** Traditional short cholis, longer peplum cholis, **straight-cut cholis, or corset-style cholis.**

● **6.5.2 Draping the Dupatta/Veil:**

o **Classic Bridal Drape:** Often pinned over the head and draped over one shoulder, or over both shoulders.

o **Double Dupatta:** A popular trend where one dupatta is draped traditionally, and a second, lighter dupatta or veil is used to cover the head.

o **Cape Style:** The dupatta or an attached sheer fabric is draped to form a cape, adding a modern, ethereal look.

o **Mixfabric's Custom Draping:** We can guide you on the best dupatta drapes that complement your chosen outfit and overall bridal vision.

● **6.5.3 Embellishment Density and Placement:**

o **All-Over Work:** Heavy embroidery covering the entire lehenga skirt and choli.

o **Border Work:** Concentrated embroidery on the borders of the lehenga and dupatta, often paired with scattered motifs on the body.

o **Buttis & Motifs:** Scattered individual motifs across the fabric for a lighter feel.

6.6 The Importance of Fit and Comfort: A Bride's Best Friend

While glamour is paramount, comfort and a perfect fit are non-negotiable for a bride on her most important day.

● **Impeccable Tailoring:** Your bridal outfit must be tailored to your precise measurements. This often involves multiple fittings, sometimes starting months in advance.

● **Freedom of Movement:** Ensure you can comfortably sit, stand, walk, and even dance in your chosen attire. You'll be wearing it for many hours, interacting with guests, and performing rituals.

• **Fabric Weight & Weather:** Consider the weight of the fabric and embellishments in relation to the weather. A heavy velvet lehenga might be uncomfortable for a summer wedding, while a light net might feel too chilly for a winter one.

• **Internal Structure:** Discuss internal corsetry, padding, and lining with your designer to ensure the outfit holds its shape and provides comfort without constant adjustment.

6.7 Beyond the Bride: Dressing for the Bridal Party and Guests

The wedding party and guests also play a crucial role in the visual grandeur of the event.

• **6.7.1 The Bridal Party (Bridesmaids/Groomsmen's Family):**

o **Coordinated Elegance:** Often, the bridal party will wear coordinated outfits or a specific color palette chosen by the couple.

o **Attire Choices:** Elegant sarees, stylish suits (palazzo/sharara), or lighter lehengas are popular choices. The level of embellishment should complement, not overshadow, the bride's attire.

• **6.7.2 Wedding Guests: Dressing Appropriately and Stylishly:**

o **Formal Indian Wedding:**

☐ **Lehengas:** Choose festive lehengas with moderate to heavy embellishments, but avoid designs that could compete with the bride's. Opt for different color palettes.

☐ **Elaborate Anarkalis:** Floor-length or heavily embellished Anarkalis in rich fabrics are perfect.

☐ **Designer Suits:** Pant suits, palazzo suits, or sharara/garara suits with intricate work.

☐ **Grand Sarees:** Silk sarees, embroidered georgette, or net sarees are always appropriate.

o **Cocktail/Reception:**

☐ **Gowns:** Elegant Western or Indo-Western gowns.

☐ **Indo-Western Fusion Wear:** Such as pant sarees, contemporary jumpsuits with ethnic touches, or sophisticated co-ord sets.

□ **Printed Silk Suits:** Comfortable and elegant.
□ **Ethnic Skirt & Kurti Sets**: Fun and versatile.
□ **Stylish Casual Ethnic Wear:** Elevated kurtis with palazzos.
○ **Rule of Thumb:** Never wear white (unless specifically requested for a theme), black (unless an evening party), or a color that matches the bride's primary wedding outfit too closely.

6.8 Accessorizing for Bridal & Wedding Looks: The Crowning Glory

Accessories elevate any bridal or wedding guest outfit, adding sparkle, tradition, and personal flair.

● **6.8.1 Bridal Jewellery:**
○ **Sets:** Bridal jewellery often includes a heavy necklace, matching earrings, maang yikka, bangles/kadas, and often a nose ring (nath), anklets (payal), and rings (haath phool).
○ **Types:** Kundan, Polki, Diamond, Gold, Temple Jewellery, or antique sets.
○ **Mixfabric's Advice:** Choose jewellery that complements your outfit's neckline and embellishments. Consider the weight and comfort for long hours.

● **6.8.2 Wedding Guest Jewellery:**
○ **Statement Pieces:** One statement necklace or a pair of heavy earrings (jhumkas, chaandbalis) can be enough.
○ **Bangles/Kadas:** A must for traditional looks.

● **6.8.3 Footwear for the Occasion:**
○ **Bridal Footwear:** Embellished heels (stilettos, block heels), wedges, or designer juttis/mojaris that are comfortable and match the outfit.
○ **Guest Footwear:** Embellished juttis, elegant flats, block heels, or strappy heels that match the formality and style of your outfit.

● **6.8.4 Clutches/Potlis:**
○ **Bridal:** A small, exquisite potli bag or an embellished clutch to carry essentials.
○ **Guest:** A chic clutch or a compact evening bag that complements your outfit.

Chapter 7: The Art of Accessorizing & Styling Secrets

An outfit is merely a canvas; accessories are the masterful strokes that bring it to life, adding personality, polish, and purpose. It's the thoughtful selection and artful placement of jewellery, bags, footwear, and even styling techniques that transform clothing from mere fabric into a cohesive, impactful statement. This chapter is your ultimate guide to mastering the nuances of accessorizing, understanding layering, curating a smart capsule wardrobe, and unlocking the secrets" that elevate your style from good to truly exceptional.

7.1 The Power of the Polish: Why Accessories Matter Most

Accessories are the unsung heroes of any wardrobe. They hold immense power to completely alter an outfit's mood, formality, and overall impression, often with minimal effort.

● **Transformative Power:** A simple white t-shirt and jeans can go from casual to chic with the right statement necklace, a structured belt, and elegant heels. A plain kurti can become festive with a vibrant dupatta and traditional jewellery.

● **Personal Expression:** Accessories are where your unique personality truly shines. They allow you to infuse trends, express your mood, and showcase your individuality without overhauling your entire wardrobe.

● **Completing the Look**: They provide the finishing touches, tying together colors, textures, and silhouettes to create a harmonious and polished ensemble.

● **Functionality Meets Fashion:** Many accessories, like bags and watches, serve practical purposes while simultaneously enhancing your style.

7.2 Jewellery: The Sparkle of Personal Style

Jewellery is perhaps the most personal of all accessories, with each piece often carrying sentimental value or reflecting cultural heritage. Mastering its selection is key to elevating your look.

● **7.2.1 Understanding Jewellery Types & Impact:**

○ **Necklaces:**

□ **Chokers:** Close-fitting, drawing attention to the neck and collarbones. Modern and chic.

□ **Pendants:** A single focal piece on a chain. Versatile for daily wear or adding subtle elegance.

□ **Statement Necklaces:** Large, ornate pieces designed to be the focal point. Best with simple necklines.

□ **Layered Necklaces:** Combining multiple delicate chains of varying lengths for a bohemian or trendy look.

□ **Traditional Indian Necklaces:** Chokers, rani haars (long necklaces), temple jewellery, Kundan, Polki, Meenakari sets – each chosen for specific ethnic outfits and formality.

o **Earrings:**
□ **Studs:** Simple, classic, and versatile for everyday.
□ **Hoops:** Classic and come in various sizes, adding a touch of casual cool or elegance.
□ **Drop Earrings:** Hang below the earlobe, ranging from delicate to dramatic.
□ **Chandelier Earrings/Jhumkas:** Multi-tiered, elaborate earrings that add significant grandeur and are quintessential for Indian ethnic wear.
□ **Chaandbalis:** Crescent moon-shaped earrings, often intricate and festive.
o **Bracelets & Bangles:**
□ **Delicate Bracelets:** For subtle sparkle and layering.
□ **Cuff Bracelets:** Bold, often sculptural pieces for a modern edge.
□ **Bangles:** Traditional Indian wrist adornments, worn singly or in sets, often symbolizing marital status or cultural identity.
□ **Kadas:** Thicker, often ornate bangles, worn singly or in pairs.
o **Rings:**
□ **Simple Bands:** Everyday elegance.
□ **Cocktail Rings:** Large, often ornate rings designed to be a statement piece.
□ **Haath Phool:** A traditional Indian hand harness, connecting a wristband to finger rings, often worn for bridal or festive occasions.
o **Anklets (Payal):** Traditional foot jewellery, particularly popular with ethnic wear, often featuring delicate bells.

● **7.2.2 Strategic Pairing for Necklines & Outfits:**
o **High Necklines (Crew, Boat, Collared):** Best with stud or drop earrings, and
bracelets. If wearing a necklace, choose a long pendant or skip it.
o **V-Necklines:** Ideal for V-shaped necklaces or pendants that follow the line of the neck, drawing the eye downwards.
o **Round/Scoop Necklines:** Perfect for chokers, shorter statement necklaces, or layered necklaces.
o **Off-Shoulder/Strapless:** Demands attention to the collarbones. Best with statement earrings and a delicate necklace or no necklace at all.

o **Heavily Embellished Outfits:** Opt for minimal jewellery (e.g., simple studs and a few bangles) to avoid an overdone look. Let the outfit shine.

o **Simple Outfits:** This is where statement jewellery truly makes an impact. Use it to add color, texture, or sparkle.

7.3 Bags: The Blend of Function and Fashion

Beyond merely holding your essentials, a bag is a powerful accessory that can elevate an outfit, define its formality, and reflect your personal style.

● **7.3.1 Types of Bags for Every Occasion:**

o **Tote Bags:** Large, open bags, perfect for daily essentials, work, or casual outings. Choose quality leather or canvas.

o **Crossbody Bags:** Hands-free and convenient, ideal for casual outings, travel, or busy days. Come in various sizes.

o **Shoulder Bags:** Versatile for daily use, work, and semi-formal events.

o **Clutches/Evening Bags:** Small, handle-less bags, perfect for parties, weddings, and formal events. Often embellished.

o **Potli Bags:** Traditional Indian drawstring bags, often embroidered or embellished, ideal for ethnic wear.

o **Backpacks (Stylish):** A modern, comfortable, and trendy choice for casual or athleisure looks.

● **7.3.2 Strategic Bag Selection:**

o **Formal Events:** Opt for sleek clutches, embellished evening bags, or small, structured top-handle bags.

o **Work/Office:** Structured shoulder bags, elegant totes, or professional satchels.

o **Casual Outings:** Crossbody bags, stylish backpacks, or large canvas totes.

7.4 Footwear: The Foundation of Your Style
Your choice of footwear impacts not just your comfort but also the entire tone and formality of your outfit.

● **7.4.1 Essential Footwear Styles:**
○ **Heels:**
□ **Stilettos:** Ultimate elegance, ideal for formal occasions.
□ **Block Heels:** More comfortable and stable, versatile for day-to-night.
□ **Wedges:** Offer height with full foot support, great for outdoor events.
□ **Kitten Heels:** Low, slender heels for a touch of elegance without extreme height.
○ **Flats:**
□ **Ballet Flats:** Classic, comfortable, and chic for daily wear.
□ **Loafers/Mules:** Polished and comfortable, great for smart casual or office wear.
□ Sandals: Open-toed, versatile for casual to semi-formal, especially in warm
weather.
□ Juttis/Mojaris: Traditional Indian embroidered flats, essential for ethnic wear.
□ Kolhapuris: Traditional Indian leather sandals, perfect for casual ethnic looks.

o **Sneakers:**

□ **Classic White Sneakers:** Universally versatile, elevate casual outfits.

□ **Fashion Sneakers:** Trendy, often colorful or chunky designs for a modern athleisure look.

● **7.4.2 Pairing Footwear with Outfits:**

o **Formal/Party Wear:** Heels (stilettos, block heels, embellished), dressy juttis (for ethnic).

o **Office/Professional:** Block heels, elegant flats, loafers, or low pumps.

o **Casual/Everyday:** Sneakers, comfortable sandals, ballet flats, or simple juttis/Kolhapuris.

o **Mixfabric's Footwear Match:** Ensure your footwear color and style complement the outfit. A nude heel elongates the leg with any dress. For traditional suits, matching juttis are key.

7.5 The Art of Layering: Adding Depth & Dimension

Layering isn't just for warmth; it's a sophisticated styling technique that adds depth, texture, and visual interest to your outfits.

● **7.5.1 Types of Layers:**

o **Inner Layers:** Camisoles, tank tops, slips, fitted turtlenecks (under dresses or blouses).

o **Mid-Layers:** Blazers, cardigans, shrugs, jackets (denim, leather), kimonos, long capes (over kurtis or dresses).

o **Outer Layers:** Coats, trench coats, heavy shawls.

● **7.5.2 Practical Layering Tips:**

o **Vary Textures:** Combine different fabrics for visual interest (e.g., a silk camisole under a linen blazer, a cotton kurti under a raw silk jacket).

o **Play with Lengths:** A longer outer layer over a shorter inner layer creates appealing proportions (e.g., a long jacket over a crop top and high-waisted pants).

o **Color Harmony:** Stick to a cohesive color palette or use a contrasting layer as a focal point.

o **Belt It:** Cinch a loose-fitting layer (like a long cardigan or an open kurti) with a belt to define your waist.

7.6 The Power of the Right Undergarments & Foundations

Often overlooked, the right foundation pieces are crucial for how your clothes look and feel.

- **Seamless Underwear:** Essential under fitted dresses, skirts, or light-colored trousers to avoid visible panty lines (VPL).
- **Bras:** The correct bra size and style (strapless, push-up, bralette, stick-on) can make or break an outfit's silhouette.
- **Shapewear:** Can smooth lines, provide support, and create a flattering silhouette under formal dresses or fitted ethnic wear like lehengas.
- **Slips/Linings:** For sheer fabrics or to prevent clinging, especially with silk or satin dresses/sarees.

7.7 Hair & Makeup: The Final Strokes

Your hair and makeup are extensions of your style, capable of transforming your look and complementing your outfit.

- **7.7.1 Hair Styling Tips:**
  o **Formal:** Sleek updos (buns, chignons), intricate braids, or Hollywood waves for a polished look.
  o **Casual:** Loose waves, ponytails, messy buns, or simple straight hair.
  o **Ethnic:** Traditional braids, elaborate buns adorned with flowers (gajra), or curls complementing ethnic jewellery.
  o **Consider Neckline:** Updos are great with high necklines or elaborate backs. Open hair works well with V-necks or off-shoulder styles.

7.8 Curating Your Capsule Wardrobe: Smart and Sustainable Style
A capsule wardrobe is a curated collection of versatile, high-quality pieces that can be mixed and matched to create numerous outfits for various occasions. It simplifies dressing, saves time, and promotes sustainable fashion.

- **7.8.1 Principles of a Capsule Wardrobe:**
o **Quality over Quantity:** Invest in durable, well-made pieces that will last.
o **Timelessness:** Focus on classic silhouettes and styles that won't quickly go out of fashion.
o **Neutral Foundation:** Build with core colors like black, white, grey, navy, and beige.
o **Accent Colors:** Add a few pieces in colors that flatter you and inject personality.
o **Versatility:** Each item should be able to combine with multiple other items in your capsule.
- **7.8.2 Building Your Mixfabric Capsule:**
o **Start with Basics:** 3-4 high-quality kurtis (Mixfabric cotton/rayon), 2-3 versatile trousers (Mixfabric palazzos/cigarette pants), 2-3 essential Western tops.
o **Add Layers:** A denim jacket, a classic blazer (Mixfabric's structured blazers).
o **Key Accessories:** A versatile bag, comfortable and dressy footwear, a few key pieces of jewellery.
o **Seasonal Refresh:** Swap out a few items each season to reflect weather and trends.
- **7.8.3 The "3-Outfit" Rule:** Before buying a new item, ask yourself if you can create at least three different outfits with existing items in your wardrobe using the new piece. If not, reconsider.

Mixfabric Style Tip: "The true art of style lies not just in what you wear, but how you wear it. By embracing the power of accessories, mastering layering, and thoughtfully curating your wardrobe, you unlock a universe of possibilities. Let Mixfabric be your partner in building a wardrobe that's not only beautiful but also intelligent, sustainable, and uniquely you." You now have the complete blueprint for mastering your style, from everyday chic to bridal grandeur. With these secrets of accessorizing and styling, you are equipped to confidently express your individuality and make a lasting impression, no matter the occasion.

MIXFABRIC

Borrow from Nature

We are passionate about being a source of inspiration for this journey. We strive to present ideas for garments that resonate with the modern woman – concepts that are beautifully designed, impeccably crafted, and effortlessly versatile. Our commitment is to provide you with the creative spark for a wardrobe that makes you feel empowered, elegant, and authentic, whether you're navigating your daily routine or celebrating life's grandest milestones. As you continue to explore, experiment, and evolve your personal style, carry these ideas and lessons with you. Let your clothes be an extension of your confidence, a testament to your taste, and a celebration of the remarkable woman you are. May your wardrobe always be a source of joy, and your style, a beacon of your individuality, fueled by endless inspiration. Embrace your style, express your story, and step into every occasion with unparalleled confidence, guided by the visions we've shared.

Conclusion

Your Style Journey, Continuously Evolving with Inspired Ideas

You've journeyed through the dynamic landscape of modern fashion, gaining inspiration for everything from the effortless charm of everyday wear to the regal splendor of bridal ensembles. We, at Mixfabric, have aimed to spark ideas and share insights into the foundational elements of a versatile wardrobe, the intricacies of Indian ethnic wear, and the transformative power of accessorizing. Our hope is that you've gained invaluable perspectives on choosing pieces that not only suit the occasion but also truly reflect your unique personality and aspirations. Remember, style isn't a destination; it's an ongoing, exhilarating journey of self-discovery and expression. The principles we've explored understanding occasion, prioritizing comfort, valuing quality craftsmanship, and embracing strategic accessorizing – are timeless concepts. They are tools to empower you to make conscious, confident choices, moving beyond fleeting trends to cultivate a wardrobe that genuinely serves you.

About the Author

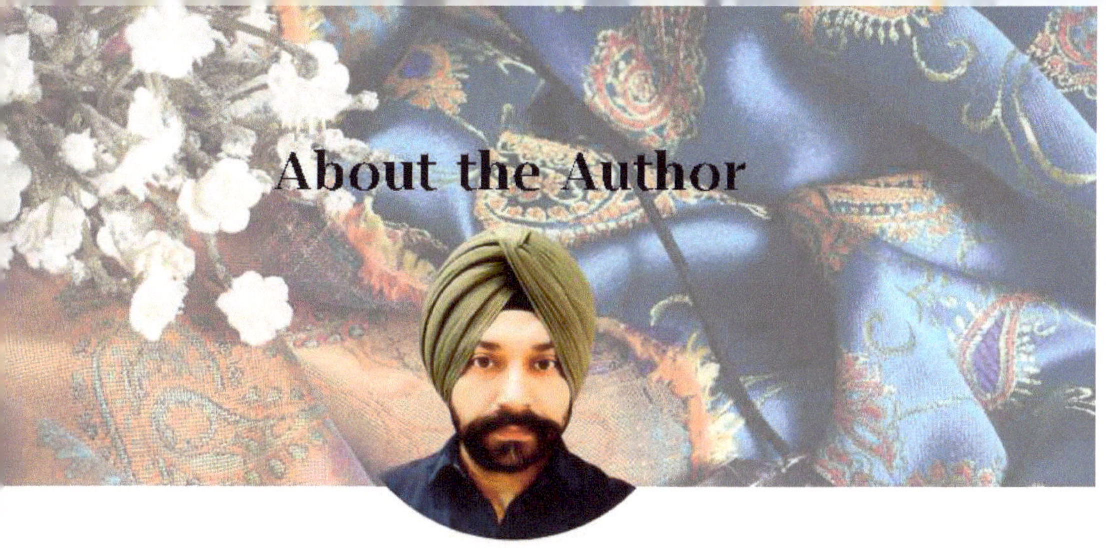

Meet Gurpuran Singh, the founder of Mixfabric, a brand synonymous with quality and the modern Indian woman's quintessential style. With a deep understanding of rich traditions and current trends, Gurpuran's Mixfabric empowers women through versatile, beautifully crafted clothing. This guide is a direct extension of his commitment to helping you build a wardrobe that radiates confidence and joy.

MIXFABRIC
Borrow from Nature

Follow the journey:
Instagram | Threads | Facebook